Editor-in-Chief and Founder:
Lyndon H. LaRouche, Jr.
Editorial Board: *Lyndon H. LaRouche, Jr. , Helga Zepp-LaRouche, Robert Ingraham, Tony Papert, Gerald Rose, Dennis Small, Jeffrey Steinberg, William Wertz*
Co-Editors: *Robert Ingraham, Tony Papert*
Managing Editor: *Nancy Spannaus*
Technology: *Marsha Freeman*
Books: *Katherine Notley*
Ebooks: *Richard Burden*
Graphics: *Alan Yue*
Photos: *Stuart Lewis*
Circulation Manager: *Stanley Ezrol*

INTELLIGENCE DIRECTORS
Counterintelligence: *Jeffrey Steinberg, Michele Steinberg*
Economics: *John Hoefle, Marcia Merry Baker, Paul Gallagher*
History: *Anton Chaitkin*
Ibero-America: *Dennis Small*
Russia and Eastern Europe: *Rachel Douglas*
United States: *Debra Freeman*

INTERNATIONAL BUREAUS
Bogotá: *Miriam Redondo*
Berlin: *Rainer Apel*
Copenhagen: *Tom Gillesberg*
Houston: *Harley Schlanger*
Lima: *Sara Madueño*
Melbourne: *Robert Barwick*
Mexico City: *Gerardo Castilleja Chávez*
New Delhi: *Ramtanu Maitra*
Paris: *Christine Bierre*
Stockholm: *Ulf Sandmark*
United Nations, N.Y.C.: *Leni Rubinstein*
Washington, D.C.: *William Jones*
Wiesbaden: *Göran Haglund*

ON THE WEB
e-mail: eirns@larouchepub.com
www.larouchepub.com
www.executiveintelligencereview.com
www.larouchepub.com/eiw
Webmaster: *John Sigerson*
Assistant Webmaster: *George Hollis*
Editor, Arabic-language edition: *Hussein Askary*

EIR (ISSN 0273-6314) *is published weekly (50 issues), by EIR News Service, Inc., P.O. Box 17390, Washington, D.C. 20041-0390. (703) 777-9451*

European Headquarters: E.I.R. GmbH, Postfach Bahnstrasse 9a, D-65205, Wiesbaden, Germany
Tel: 49-611-73650
Homepage: http://www.eirna.com
e-mail: eirna@eirna.com
Director: Georg Neudecker

Montreal, Canada: 514-461-1557

Denmark: EIR - Danmark, Sankt Knuds Vej 11, basement left, DK-1903 Frederiksberg, Denmark. Tel.: +45 35 43 60 40, Fax: +45 35 43 87 57. e-mail: eirdk@hotmail.com.

Mexico City: EIR, Sor Juana Inés de la Cruz 242-2 Col. Agricultura C.P. 11360 Delegación M. Hidalgo, México D.F. Tel. (5525) 5318-2301 eirmexico@gmail.com

Canada Post Publication Sales Agreement #40683579

Postmaster: Send all address changes to *EIR*, P.O. Box 17390, Washington, D.C. 20041-0390.

Signed articles in *EIR* represent the views of the authors, and not necessarily those of the Editorial Board.

What Is the Nature of Man?

EIR Contents

www.larouchepub.com Volume 43, Number 17, April 22, 2016

What Is the Nature of Man?

Cover This Week

Detail of Rembrandt self-portrait, 1659, oil on canvas

National Gallery of Art, Washington, D.C./Steven Zucker

I. The World Land-Bridge

HELGA ZEPP-LAROUCHE

Historic Aims of the Schiller Institute's April 7, 2016 Manhattan Conference

At a moment in history when the world is shaken by rising military tensions in many corners of the Earth; a new looming financial crisis, worse than that of 2008; an extremely upsetting refugee crisis in Europe, as the result of a series of wars in Southwest Asia based on lies; an apparently endless number of scandals pertaining to criminal aspects of the international system, such as the Panama Papers or the classified 28 pages of the 9/11 Congressional report,—it is clear that we are dealing with a civilizational crisis.

It should also be evident to any thinking person, that a continuation of the present practices in all likelihood will lead to a human catastrophe, of which the two World Wars of the Twentieth Century gave a foretaste of potential things to come. In the age of thermonuclear weapons, this would very probably mean the annihilation of the human civilization.

However, mankind is the only creative species known so far, and therefore has the potential to find solutions to all challenges by discovering new principles, deeper understandings of the lawfulness of our universe, and answers on a higher level of reason than the level on which the conflict arose. Gottfried Wilhelm Leibniz insisted in the Seventeenth Century, that man has the unique power to answer a great evil with an even greater good.

If we are going to escape the present dangers, we have to reject almost all of the axioms of today's methods of thinking and popular culture. We have to replace them with a completely new paradigm, defined by the future of humanity as one, and the common aims of mankind, rather than geopolitical confrontations. We need to base this new paradigm on the optimistic image of man as limitless and perfectible, both intellectually and morally. If we think thousands and thousands of years into the future, the true identity of man will be that of genius.

The Schiller Institute is conducting a series of international conferences with the aim of bringing together forces from all over the world to establish joint partner-

EIRNS/Stuart Lewis

Helga Zepp-LaRouche participating in Panel I of the April 7 Schiller Institute Conference in New York City.

ships for development, such as are already progressing with the New Silk Road initiated by China. In collaboration with *EIR*, the Schiller Institute is promoting the idea that *The New Silk Road Becomes the World Land-Bridge,* as a very concrete program to overcome poverty on all continents, starting with the necessary infrastructure development as the precondition for the development of industry and agriculture.

But it is also evident that this new paradigm of an economic development perspective for the whole world can only succeed if it is combined with a renaissance of Classical culture, which can inspire the necessary creativity and aesthetic transformation of the people. An absolutely essential feature of these conferences is therefore a dialogue of the high phases of the different cultures, to make people more conscious of the enormous richness of universal history and the profound beauty of our world and our universe.

This issue of EIR *continues the coverage of that April 7 conference which we began in our previous issue. Part I of this issue covers more fully the conference's first panel, on the World Land-Bridge. Part II covers the third and final panel, on the inner unity shared by all of mankind's most advanced Classical cultures.*

AMBASSADOR AHMED FAROUK

The New Suez Canal in the World Land-Bridge

Ambassador Ahmed Farouk is the Egyptian Consul General in New York. He spoke at the Schiller Institute conference in New York, April 7.

Dennis Speed: President Franklin Roosevelt, working with Harry Hopkins, Frances Perkins, Henry Wallace, and others, put millions of Americans to work in what Roosevelt called the New Deal. Recently, the spirit of FDR reappeared in the form of the government of Egypt, which has accomplished something which was considered by many people to be impossible. Here to tell you how the apparently impossible was done, in record time, is Ambassador Ahmed Farouk, the Consul General of Egypt in New York. Please join me in welcoming him.

Ambassador Farouk: Good morning, distinguished guests. I would like to thank the Schiller Institute, represented by Mrs. Helga Zepp-LaRouche, the founder of the Institute, and also I would like to acknowledge the role of economist Lyndon LaRouche, the founder and editor of *Executive Intelligence Review*, for convening this important conference. My remarks today will be very brief, about the history and the new initiative of the Silk Road, and I will focus on the project of the Suez Canal in Egypt, which connects the Silk Road east and west.

First, the history. Throughout history, humans have always moved from one place to another, exchanging goods, skills, and ideas. Eurasia remains always the criss-crossing center for communication routes and paths of trade, which gradually became known as the

EIRNS/Stuart Lewis

Ambassador Ahmed Farouk, Counsel General of Egypt in New York.

Silk Road. The history of these routes can be traced back thousands of years. Egypt, with its approximately seven thousand years of history, has long been at the center of global commerce, and at the axis of trade routes linking Europe, Asia, and Africa. Two branches of the Old Silk Road intersected Egyptian maritime and caravan routes.

Recently, there have been many attempts to revive the ancient Silk Road. The most recent attempt came from China, when the Chinese President formally announced in 2013 the Silk Road Economic Belt, and subsequently expanded the program to include the Maritime Silk Road. The program aims to unlock massive trade potential and bolster economic development through the so-called Belt. The project consists of two main components: the land-based Silk Road Economic Belt, and the Maritime Silk Road. The first one links China with Europe through Central and Western Asia, and the second one, the maritime, is designed to connect China with Southeast Asia, Africa, and Europe.

Egypt plays a major role in that belt, due to its strategic geographic location, as a land-bridge between Asia and Africa, and a link between two principal waterways: the Mediterranean Sea and the Indian Ocean. This inevitably makes it a pivotal country on the crossroads between Asia, Africa, and Europe, and an important partner for the major and emerging powers. In January 2016, Egypt and China signed a memorandum of understanding on the New Silk Road Economic Belt and the 21st Century Maritime Silk Road.

The New Suez Canal and Its Corridor

Now I will go to the New Suez Canal project, the magic words of international commerce. It is recorded that Egypt was the first country to dig a manmade canal across its lands with a view to activating the world of trade. The idea of linking the Mediterranean Sea with the Red Sea by means of a canal, dates back forty centuries. When the Suez Canal was inaugurated in 1869, it changed the course of global transport by shortening the route between Europe and Asia approximately 7,000

CCTV America

An early phase in the construction for doubling the capacity of the Suez Canal in Egypt, shown here in China TV coverage. The expansion project was completed in late July 2015 after one year.

miles, which made it the shortest link between East and West. For Egypt, the Suez Canal is not only a national asset. It is a natural resource, a unique boon that generates steady income and ensures Egypt international standing. And it is enough to know that approximately 20 percent of global shipping passes through this canal.

Bringing the approximately 150-year-old canal to the 21st Century, President Sisi of Egypt, in August 2014, launched the New Suez Canal mega-project, involving an expansion of the existing canal, and the development of its environs into a global trade hub. This expansion included establishing a new, parallel waterway approximately 35 miles long, and additionaly deepening and widening 35 miles of the existing canal. This allowed two-way traffic, cutting the time of every vessel passing through the canal by half, from 22 hours to 11 hours. The new canal cost $8 billion: $4 billion for the excavation and construction, and $4 billion for tunnels linking Sinai with the mainland of Egypt. The government invited the Egyptian public to participate in this project through tax-free investment certificates offered by the state-owned banks. Surprisingly and amazingly, the certificates sold out in less than ten days, and the government generated $8 billion in exactly nine days.

The principle behind the idea of the project of the New Suez Canal was that Egypt needed a project which would support the national economy, making use of the existing potential to create a well-developed industrial

zone. We need to provide job opportunities, while creating new urban communities to attract youth to the canal zone, based on the growth of world trade in places such as China, Southeast Asia and India, and going to Europe and the United States via the Suez Canal. Since the project began, over 43,000 Egyptians have worked on it. They moved in total half a trillion cubic meters of earth. By our Egyptian measures, we say it is equivalent to 200 Great Pryamids in one year. The new canal was inaugurated in August 2015. Revenues are expected to increase from about $5.3 billion a year in 2015 to $13.2 billion in 2020.

The new canal project goes apace with the Suez Canal Corridor Development Project, a development zone which will turn Egypt into an international logistics center. The new industrial zones aim to develop over 400 square miles, including six ports on the Mediterranean Sea and the Gulf of Suez, to provide a service hub centered on the canal activities. They are expected to add about one million new jobs for Egyptians and others, particularly focussed on youth, and to support the local economy. The Suez Canal Corridor Development Project is the centerpiece of an aggressive development perspective with implications for all Northeast Africa, Southeast Asia, and the Maritime Silk Road. It is a message of hope for a better future to the youth and the coming generation in Egypt, the Middle East, and Africa. It aims at better understanding, more tolerance, and peaceful co-existence.

RAMSEY CLARK

The Idea of Justice Is Still Alive

Ramsey Clark, U.S. Attorney General 1967-1969, spoke at the Schiller Institute conference in New York, April 7.

Dennis Speed: There was a time in the United States when the citizens of this country appealed to their government for justice, and their government would respond. This was the time of the Roosevelt Administration of the 1940s and the time of the Kennedy Administration of 1961-63. Next May we will celebrate the 100th birthday of JFK. That was the last period, the 1960s, when the United States really was still a society striving toward justice, although it was a highly imperfect nation. Now this man, whose humility is undeserved, is one of the last expressions of that time of justice. Whether we are talking about his protection of Martin Luther King on the march from Selma to Montgomery, 51 years ago in Alabama, or his opposition to the Iraq wars of 1991 and 2003, his defense of controversial personages in his legal practice, or his speaking out in any case of injustice upon which his attention falls, he has distinguished himself by insisting on the truth. He still represents the idea of justice in the United States and, as with Socrates in Athens, as long as he is in the United States, and here in New York City in particular, the idea of justice is still alive in the United States. Please join me in welcoming to the podium former Attorney General of the United States Ramsey Clark.

Peace and the Elimination of Poverty

Ramsey Clark: Thank you, thank you. Well, what a good audience and gathering in the cause of peace, and

EIRNS/Stuart Lewis

Ramsey Clark: "We ought to look forward to the challenge with joy."

the elimination of poverty, and the address to the last true remaining challenges to humanity, and living in peace together on mother Earth. We are not very good children. We mistreat our mother in more ways than we really understand.

Late last year I flew from north to south in Korea and from north to south in Viet Nam, and the devastation that was wreaked on those two countries in the last century is still so manifest. You look at areas where Agent Orange was mindlessly deployed, and you have what could only be called a vast wasteland, more than a wasteland; it is not healthy to be there, after all these years. The amount of money that we spent, the vastness of our national involvement in the projects, if you want to call it that, and the death and destruction, both physically and, not easily measured, but clearly morally as well, is undeterminable.

We have a vast challenge still in defining how, and living by, principles that will ensure peace. It will take us out of the laboratory where mad scientists are still trying to find better and more efficient means of mass destruction, to where we have a society that is more interested in the welfare of our children than the status of our national defense, which is a corruption of the word defense, because it really implies just the opposite, the power to coerce others by the threat or use of superior technology and mass destruction, and superior forces committed to its deployment.

The planet is still habitable in spite our strenuous efforts, but if we keep on, we may wake up one morning and find that mother Earth is sick, that we are the cause of the sickness, and that if we don't love our mama, we'll pay a heavy price.

The Happiest Challenge

The challenge of addressing what is a crisis, is really one of the happiest challenges that a population ever had. It ought to be a lot more fun than developing new technology for mass destruction, because it's how not only to preserve, but to improve the natural condition of the planet, a beautiful planet which offers peace and prosperity for all, and yet, because of our lusts and our conduct, still faces the possibility of mass destruction.

It amazes me how science,— I

GFDL/Mohammed Tanvirul Islam
Street child at Srimangal Railway Station, Bangladesh.

always enjoyed science, because I thought it was our effort to better understand all aspects of the, not only global, but planetary and interplanetary environment in which we live; there's a great adventure still possible on this planet, and more interesting, in a way, at least in terms of its unknown aspects now, and mastery of the universe beyond. The biggest challenge we have is as simple as how to live together with love and affection and constructive conduct within our family and among our neighbors and across our nation, and most importantly of all, with peace and constructive interaction with all of the other neighbors that share the planet that still remains preponderantly beautiful, but has growing wastelands because of our thoughtless and careless and dangerous abuse of what we call mother nature.

We have the capacity to solve all of our problems; we engage more in creating problems, however, with more of our resources and the greater part of our energies and sadly, even our aspirations, in how we dominate the globe by the threat and use of violence, which a loving people would have prevented and overcome long ago. But look at the size of the militaries, look at the continuing investment in the discovery and creation, sometimes, of the development and utilization— by threat and by actual deployment—of the means we now have of mass destruction. Military budgets abandoned and transformed into education and food production and housing and family protection in Asia, and Africa, and Latin America will transform the quality of life on the planet; and still we are spending billions on

forms of violence and the threat of their use to cause others to act as we want them to, in ways that are not good for their children, or ours either.

Until we violate what seems to be our major commitment to a superior capacity for violence, until we recognize its threat to our present and future, to our children, until we eliminate means of mass destruction and the will to tolerate them—to accept them as a presence in our midst—then we live in danger of the chance of our own conduct ending, or vastly impairing, the capacity for future generations to live in peace, with prosperity. Which doesn't take too much, it means just the right amount to overcome our lust for acquisition and to enjoy the things that are really beneficial, really important, assuring the health and the well-being and education of all children everywhere, all adults and senior folks, like me, everywhere, employing our wits, such as they be, and our energies, which are clearly sufficient, if properly employed, to assure for every child born on Earth health and education and the opportunity to fully develop all of their potential for individual contribution to their own well-being and the well-being of their families and the well-being of the rest of us.

A Challenge You Can Really Enjoy

Now that is a challenge you can really enjoy, a lot more than working in the laboratory for development of the technology for mass destruction, even if that technology seems to be beneficial, but in fact is destroying the environment that is necessary for the continuation of life on the planet. If human nature likes challenges, and I have to admit to great affection for challenges—they interest me more than anything else around—then we will accept these challenges and we can overcome the suffering, the vast suffering, that is seen in any travel through poverty in the United States itself, but also vast parts of Africa, and Asia, and Latin America. If our real time and energies and desires were directed toward the quality of life—which means the quality of life of the planet, as well as of the living creatures here, crawling around on it—we will not only not become the first species to destroy itself, and probably take most of the others with us: Maybe some other forms will come along that won't have such a lust for belligerency.

We need to face why it is that we still have scientists spending billions on the search for better means of mass destruction, the manufacture of the technology that can consume us with its product of mass destruction, when we are way behind on how we raise healthy and happy children and unified families, not only where we live, which is, because of our affluence, not so much a challenge as it is in most parts of the world.

We have an interest, a human interest, an important interest that is essential to the future on the planet, of ensuring health for all the children of the planet, most of whom have no insurance, either the corporate kind or just the human availability kind. They have mother love, but where mother is hungry and sick herself, her capacities are limited. And yet, when you go around the world, you see a larger suffering than the size of those who are celebrating an excess of affluence.

It's one of the most interesting challenges that humanity has ever had, one of the most difficult certainly, one of the greatest, simply because of the numbers in the game today, but if we really enlist for the duration,— in a commitment to improving the quality of life globally for all people, in eliminating not only militarism, but the threat of all forms of violence toward humanity, the most dangerous of which may be not militarism now, but the threat to the environment.

We have a beautiful planet. It was given to us free of charge, and it requires some tending, and yet what you could call, in our system, "the profit motive," not only pays no attention to the well-being of mother Earth, but exploits her, because the bottom line doesn't require

Slums built on swamp land near a garbage dump in East Cipinang, Jakarta, Indonesia.

you to invest in the preservation of the environment and the productivity of the soil and, above all, the knowledge, understanding, and commitment of the people to a life of freedom and peace on the planet.

I travel too much—a sane person wouldn't do it—and I don't travel to happy places very often. I may pass through the airport at Paris, but I'm on my way to Bangladesh, or someplace where the human condition is not acceptable, where mere safety itself is never secure, not to mention food, and health care, and education. We have a vast challenge.

It is hard to imagine, though, a greater source of joy that people of conscience could have, than putting your shoulder to the wheel to see that we are committed wisely—and with sufficient knowledge to know the consequences of our acts—to the preservation of life on the planet and the opportunity for all of the children yet to come, to enjoy a continually better condition than the condition in which we will leave it.

Mother Earth has deep scars from our conduct, and you can see them in cities and in the countryside of even the most prosperous nations. But you go to the continents where so many of the poor people live, to Africa and many parts of our own hemisphere, to parts of Asia, where vast millions and millions live without adequate health care, meaningful education, decent housing, or even decent food.

If you like challenge, then we live in the best of all times, because we have the greatest challenge and the clear potential to address and resolve all threats to the human condition on the planet. There is no need for children to die in infancy, or live in malnutrition and die young, and live with no peace and security—and yet it's a constant threat to a major part of, if not most, of those of us who live currently in the third world, and even here, even in a great city like New York, there are children raised in conditions of poverty and neglect that are unacceptable to a humane concern.

Miles to Go Before We Sleep

Though the woods may be lovely, dark and deep, we have promises to keep, and miles to go before we sleep. But we need to recognize that we're on the road, that we're in a race between catastrophe and education— the deployment of what education tells us is essential for life, human life on the planet, in the century just ahead.

It won't be an easy time. We're pretty comfortable here, but if you look around, the real dangers are vast, and particularly in the environmental sector, we're losing ground. They're not recognized, and the people who endure the worst conditions are those with the least capacity to do anything about it, so it takes those with the greater capacity to come to the rescue of all of us, because on this small planet, with its huge population now, we are literally in the same boat, brother. As the old song went, when you shake one end, you're going to rock the other.

So, those of us here who have had such a unique opportunity for knowledge, for a life of peace, for the opportunity to see what's possible, we've got to pull our socks up and enjoy the most important struggle that humanity has faced, and that is how to live in peace, with a growing population.

We ought to look forward to the challenge with joy; we are lucky to have important work. All we have to do is recognize it, roll up our sleeves, and do it. This is the true joy of life; the joy, as Saul said, is in being deeply involved in a cause that you yourself deem mighty, being fairly worn out before you are thrown on the scrap heap. It is in seizing the opportunity to help our children, in a world that we have contributed to, to overcome the many challenges to live in a future of peace and plenty, where love permeates all the societies within themselves and among each other.

JAI POONG RYU

The New Silk Road and Korean Unification

Jai Poong Ryu, of the One Korea Foundation, delivered this presentation at the April 7 Schiller Institute Conference in New York City.

Dennis Speed: United States troops have been stationed in Korea since about 1950; there are still about 28,000 U.S. troops there. Korea is still divided. Why? With the possibility of Russian, Chinese, and American cooperation never being more obvious than in Korea's case, would not the reunification of Korea, like the reunification of Germany, be a possible opportunity for a new era in world diplomacy?

The next speaker offers a perspective for unification: peace through development. Please join me in welcoming Prof. Jai Poong Ryu, retired from Loyola College, who is the founder of the One Korea Foundation.

Jai Poong Ryu: Thank you very much. I consider this to be quite an honor, personally and otherwise, to be invited to speak at this very important and timely Schiller Institute conference this year.

Helga LaRouche spoke of the need to go beyond the geopolitical considerations and polarity, and that's a very timely comment, because of the geopolitical considerations of the powers beyond Koreans' control that caused us to be divided, 71 years ago. It was the geopolitical consideration of disarming the Japanese Imperial Army north of the 38th parallel by the Sovi-

EIRNS/Stuart Lewis
Professor Jai Poong Ryu, of the One Korea Foundation, advocated the unification of Korea, and identified the pitfalls to be avoided, in his address to the April 7, 2016 Schiller Institute Conference.

ets, who had just entered the peninsula, and south of that parallel by United States forces, which came a little later.

We remained divided for 70 years, and the geopolitical considerations of the world continue to keep the peninsula divided. Now it is time to pay some attention to that.

Attorney General Ramsey Clark talked about many global issues—environment, poverty, income disparity—but alongside all of these problems is also the problem that there is nobody really talking about the Korea issue, or thinking about it. The many problems we have may seem to be enough, but nobody is really addressing the Korea issue, which is very depressing.

I admire the accomplishments of this Schiller Institute, and I hope to convey some ideas about Korea, so that you can somehow find some link between what you are also after, that is, a World Land-Bridge, and how it might have some implications for Korean unification.

Since my retirement four years ago, my time and attention have been devoted to Korean unification. This goal of Korean unification, however, is unlike some other things I have done. It is not really a goal-oriented endeavor, but is more a long-term direction-oriented endeavor. Because I will be 75 years old in October of this year—and if I have a lifetime goal that I want to implement in the next five years, it will be too depressing to see the reality. The indicators are too discouraging and frustrating, and I may actually give up before I start.

Instead, I have to think about a more general direction we want to move in, and I will just carry it out as far as I can go and let my effort stop there, and then let the issue follow along. So it is more in that spirit that I do what I do. Because, once Korean unification is mentioned, in and out of Korea *per se,* there is a plethora, a whole gamut of opinions. On the one hand, you have people who think that unification is not desirable. They think that the status quo is quite beneficial. All the powers around Korea seem to think so.

China intervened in the Korean War out of geopolitical considerations, not wanting to be confronted with American forces across the Yalu River. And that continues to this day.

Japan finds that South Korea's emerging industrial power is strong enough to rival them. Therefore, to them, a unified Korea is not welcome news.

The United States, too, does not find unification particularly desirable. And there are some sinister interpretations that there is a hidden hand in the United States that likes to keep Korea divided, so that Koreans can continue to buy arms, guns, and tanks, and that there are people who make money from that. I don't know. I have never really looked into it. Actually, with all the scholarship devoted to it, there have been very few figures, numbers, or tables produced to demonstrate that. So the rumor, whether it's really true or not, continues.

Comparison with German Unification

And there are people who believe, especially comparing Korea's situation to Germany, that Korea has been divided for 70 years, but it's only been since German unification that the idea of Korean unification has become a little more real to Korean people. But then, if we compare East and West Germany to North and South Korea, the signs are more depressing. West Germany was much richer than South Korea, much bigger than East Germany—*vis-à-vis* East Germany to West Germany; it was three times the size. North and South Korea land-wise are about the same; the population of South Korea is twice that of North Korea. So West Germany was much richer than East Germany.

You know, at the time of German unification, East and West Germans sent letters to each other, there were telephone calls, they exchanged Christmas cards, they

Map of North and South Korea. The combined territory of the two is approximately equal to the size of Utah. South Korea has a population of about 50 million, while North Korea has a population of about 25 million.

visited each other. Nothing like that has happened in Korea. The recent divided families, at one time some 10 million individuals, about a quarter of that number of families being the number of families involved, remained divided. And when they tried to give them a three-day reunion, it took three years of preparation, and it's a terrible thing.

So, when we compare the Korea situation to Germany, the idea is that we cannot afford it. The West German economy suffered from it, and even today in Germany, there are people called "Ossies" and "Wessies" [Easterners and Westerners], and there is prejudice, and all the blame tends to be placed on something that went wrong through the reunification process. Korea doesn't want to repeat that, and we definitely cannot afford it.

On the other side, there are people who believe that unification is not desirable because the status quo is not too bad, both internationally and domestically.

South Korea was an impoverished nation! When I left Korea in 1965, per-capita income was $100 per person [per year], at the level of perhaps Uganda or Rwanda in Africa today. Today, South Korea is by some measures the 10th to 14th largest economy in the world—and about half the size of Utah.

That's a remarkable accomplishment. In the post-World War II period, since 1945, South Korea is the only country, that out of *utter* dirt poverty, accomplished a true industrialization and democratization—it's a proud heritage.

So, now we can make a living. We don't have beggars any more, we don't

Augmented by an industrialization drive beginning in the late 1960s, South Korea went from dirt poor to an economy that ranks from 10th to 14th largest in the world. By 2014, South Korea was the seventh largest exporter and seventh largest importer in the world. Here, a Hyundai Heavy Industries shipyard in South Korea, 2014.

have starving people any more. We don't have a budget that relies 60% or 70% on American foreign aid. We *give* foreign aid, we help many parts of the underdeveloped world. So, we can now live. But if Korea is suddenly united, South Koreans are afraid that we will then have to guarantee the basic livelihood of 25 million people. We can't afford that. There are people who believe we cannot afford that. They think status quo is therefore not so bad.

On the other side, there are people who believe in "unification at all costs" no matter what, even if it takes some bloodshed. They think unification is a must, that Korea was always a unified country, one people, one land, and it must be put together again.

What Kind of Unification?

I don't belong to either camp. I want to see—and I speak for the One Korea Foundation—a particular kind of unification. If Korea somehow united through military means, or through a sudden collapse of the Kim family, the dynasty of the regime, then the chaos would be such that there would be no force, no personal or

leadership caliber that could possibly control this. Therefore, without great preparation, a painful, gradual, solid effort on the part of both South Korea and North Korea, closely supported and coordinated internationally, with the involvement of China, the United States, Japan, and Russia—arguably the four greatest powers of the world—Korean unification would not be possible.

What kind of Korean unification do we want? Korean unification must be done by the Korean people. We will not ask other people to do it. Although we were divided by others, we will unify ourselves. But we cannot do it alone, definitely not! Especially if anyone is actively opposed to it. Even in a very illustrative presentation by Professor Li of the Silk Road, there is one country that's not mentioned—Bangladesh, Pakistan, Tibet, Kazakhstan, Xinjiang are mentioned; but not a word of Korea. China calls itself the Middle Kingdom, and now, in the Silk Road concept it defines itself as if it's the Far East, not the Middle any more. In order to be Middle, it had better include Korea.

What Unification Will Mean to Koreans

When Koreans think of unification, newspaper columnists and college professors talk about what unification will bring to Korea. Korea is a peninsula. But South Korea has been a virtual *island*: Three sides sea, and the Demilitarized Zone. We have been living on an island for 70 years. So one dream for the unification of Korea into one, is somehow an idea that college freshmen and sophomores will take a backpack and get on a cross-continental Eurasian railroad, and go all the way to Madrid, to Venice, and they get excited about that. This is one of the ingredients of the dream that is keeping unification alive in the minds of the young people in Korea.

Michael Billington was so good as to have a copy of my Declaration for Unification prepared for you—do you all have it? I would be very honored if you would take the time to read it. It is not much of a document of literature, perhaps, but it took me seven months to write it, to revise it, to change every word—every word! I must have spent hours on it. So, just take pity on me, and have a good read.

Now, the type of unification we want is not really that easy. It takes some very, very specific measures. When Korea is united, the basic idea is that people will travel south in search of a better standard of living. Money will travel north in search of profit. How many people will come down? How much money will go north? These questions are a kind of mathematical equation. There is some formula there. For ten years at least, after unification, South Korea and North Korea must be run as two economic zones.

Helmut Kohl of West Germany made three mistakes at the time of German unification, and they told us so. And we've learned a great deal from the German experience, and hopefully will not repeat the same mistakes.

One is that they equalized the wage structure of East and West Germany, and declared that the deutschemark of the two countries was of the same value. Secondly, Helmut Kohl also made it possible for West Germans who had lost property in East Germany to reclaim it. They said, in the ten years after German unification, 230,000 lawsuits were filed in the German courts, so Korea must not repeat that mistake. So, we will have to be very careful about this.

The third is a very tough call. We have to persuade the international community that for a ten-year period after unification, there should be a Bi-Korea policy, instead of the resources, the hardware, and the capital for the infrastructure building of North Korea—including the building of power plants, roads, railroads, refurbishing harbors, and so on—only coming from South Korea. Otherwise, it will be very, very difficult. The Korean economy is just not as a big as that of Germany. We will not be able to sustain it, and I may regret that I talked about unification, considering what we have brought up here.

The One Korea Foundation at this time has a very limited purpose. Last year in commemoration of our seventh anniversary, we held a big banquet in the Senate caucus room, and held a big rally at the Lincoln Memorial, whose legacy we want to borrow: "With malice toward none, with charity for all," in Lincoln's second Inaugural Address: That is the spirit in which we want to unify our country.

So, in one of our first efforts, we have to come to what we call AOL—American Opinion Leaders—and they're found in the business world, in academia, in the press. We would like to be a sort of top-notch website in the next couple years or so, so that this is the site these opinion leaders come to when questions about unification arise.

And we want to redefine the United States-Republic of Korea alliance so that it will cover security measures not just involving U.S. and Korea. The R.O.K.-U.S. alliance is based on the idea that the United States will come to the defense of South Korea against North Korean aggression. It presupposes the division! The whole alliance is premised on the fact that the country is divided and will continue to be divided. We must find—as Helga LaRouche pointed out—we must find a formula beyond that. The U.S.-R.O.K. alliance must not be for defense only, but for one Korea, for Korean unification. It remodels all issues in a different type of framework.

And I think President Xi Jinping very much included Korea in his talk with President Park about his proposed New Silk Road. So, maybe next time, Professor Li will bring his students to visit Korea, the easternmost end of the Silk Road and World Land-Bridge. In my view, the World Land-Bridge starts with Korean unification. And as some friends once said: Let there be peace on Earth, and let it begin here, with us, with Korean unification.

The Folly of U.S. Military Interventions in Iraq, Syria, and Libya Since 2011

This is a transcript of a video presentation by Virginia State Senator Richard Black to the April 7, 2016 Schiller Institute conference.

Senator Richard Black: I'm Senator Dick Black, State Senator of Virginia. I have a long military history. I fought with the First Marine Regiment in Vietnam and also flew helicopters on quite a number of missions, so I'm very pro-military, but at the same time I have very deep reservations about what we're doing in Syria.

So, I'd like to talk with you, and I'd like to just give you a rundown on where we stand today and kind of how we got there. Syria is the essential nation in the Middle East, because everything revolves around Syria.

What I will present is a brief countdown to the Syrian war. There are things that preceded it, obviously. But I want to just start with 2001.

In 2001, the Pentagon started war-planning to topple the Syrian government. [Gen.] Wesley Clark said that after the 9/11 attacks he was in the Pentagon, visiting with the Secretary of Defense, and then he went and he spoke with a friend of his who was a general, and the general said, "Boss, you got to look at this." Clark said, "What is it?"

He said, "We're going to attack Iraq!" And General Clark said, "Why? Have we found something on weapons of mass destruction?" The general said, "No, it looks like we just figured we got a great military, and we got a problem, and we're going to do something with it."

About a month later, General Clark goes back in, and he looks up this same general. He says, "Is it still on? Are we still going to attack Iraq?" And the general said, "Hey, it's worse than that," and he pulled up a sheet of paper. He said, "we've got plans now to topple seven governments in the Middle East." Now, one of them was Syria. One of them was also Libya, which

ties in with Syria, so I want to discuss both. But in any event, the war-planning had clearly begun in 2001.

Now, what's important about 2001? Well, the Syrian war did not begin until 10 years later. There were no uprisings in Syria. The Syrians were prosperous. It was one of the most prosperous nations in the Middle East, one of the most advanced. Syria had the greatest women's rights and the greatest religious freedom of any of the Arab nations. Think about that. Here, we've demonized Syria, and yet, they were the nation that had genuine freedom relative to all of the other Arab nations.

So we begin war-planning in 2001. WikiLeaks did a tremendous service, I think, to all of us, when it released some of the diplomatic communiqués out of the Syrian Embassy. A communiqué from the U.S. Embassy in 2006 described a detailed plan for destabilizing and undermining the Syrian government.

The year 2011 becomes a very terrible year in Mideast history. This is when the so-called "Arab Spring" starts in Tunisia and then, all of a sudden, unrest spontaneously occurs in so many countries, as it often does when covert operatives go to work. The United States, Britain, and France took the lead, working together with Turkey, and with Qatar, and we promoted the Libyan uprising.

Now, why did we do this? Colonel Qaddafi had become the principal ally of the United States in the war on terror in North Africa. We had had our problems with him, to be sure, but they had been settled. We had normalized relations.

We went in there, and with the great help of Senator John McCain, we declared that there would be a "no fly zone." Now, a "no fly zone" is a strange name for a "free fire zone," but that's what it is. It's a free fire zone, where you go in and you literally bomb everything to smithereens. That's what we did.

By the time that we were finished in Libya, there essentially was no government, there was no culture, there was *nothing*. Everything was destroyed except for the Libyan arms supplies. Colonel Qaddafi had a vast supply of modern arms.

The purpose in overthrowing Libya was to be able to take these advanced weapons from Libya, send them through Turkey into Syria, to overthrow Syria. And this was their way of getting around having to go to Congress for appropriations, and having to say, "Hey, look, Congress. Let's go in and let's attack an allied nation, a neutral, non-belligerent country, and murder its leader. What d'ya think?" I don't think they'd have gotten very far. It's much easier to simply stage a covert operation, and so that's what happened there.

This is the outline of where we were and how we got there.

The Syrian war is often presented as a domestic uprising, an uprising of people who wanted freedom and democracy. A Defense Intelligence Agency study that was commissioned by the Joint Chiefs of Staff determined that this is essentially a myth, this idea of "moderate rebels." It has always been a myth. The Syrian rebels were heavily infiltrated and controlled by the terrorists from the very beginning.

Saudi-Turkish Sponsorship of Terrorism

Now, what I'd like to do is go beyond that. If you go back to early in 2015, what had happened is the Turks and the Saudis had teamed up and they had formed something called the Army of Conquest. The Army of Conquest was based and centered around al-Nusra. Al-Nusra is al-Qaeda in Syria, and al-Qaeda, you'll recall, is the group that killed 3,000 Americans when they attacked the Twin Towers and the Pentagon on 9/11. So Turkey and Saudi Arabia put together this Army of Conquest, based on the *very people* who carried out the greatest attack ever on the American homeland.

Turkey runs along the northern border of both Syria and Iraq. Now what this map shows you here, the green portions are now controlled by the Kurds. You recall the heroic battle at Kobane? I have spoken to Kurds who were present on the Turkish side of the border. The Turkish army had protected the border with tanks, they put in 50 tanks. During the battle of Kobane, the Turks

from Senator Richard Black's video message

Virginia Senator Richard Black, in a video message he sent to the April 7 Schiller Institute conference in New York City.

brought convoys of Red Crescent ambulances, which is like the Red Cross in the Middle East, and they loaded them with ISIS jihadis and they used the ambulances, which the Kurds obviously would not fire on, and they used them to carry ammunition and fresh troops into battle for ISIS. So this was going on.

Well, what happened was the Kurds finally managed to get the best of ISIS. They conquered ISIS and, rather than simple securing Kobane, they began to attack, and they began to move all the way across the border, and they began to seal it and to cut off access to Turkey.

This threatened to totally block access from ISIS. Now, the number-one ally of ISIS is Turkey. Turkey provides them with all of the arms, with all the ammunition, with hospitals to treat their wounded. They have regular routes where jihadists from all over the world are recuited and come in. They pay various rebels both in al-Qaeda and ISIS. Now, Turkey supplies the Army of Conquest, which is al-Qaeda based, through this gap over here, which they have opened up. But this Kobane gap is where ISIS is supplied.

Now, if you look at the gray area, the gray area is held by ISIS. ISIS has, or they did have, 1,200 oil tankers that were running oil through the Kobane gap— 44,000 barrels of oil a day were transiting through there, and unlike the typical border controls that Turkey has over things flowing through, they wave the oil through. They knew what that was, and they knew where it was going. And it was going on the market, and they paid good money to ISIS. This was probably the major single source of financing for ISIS. But it wasn't the only one.

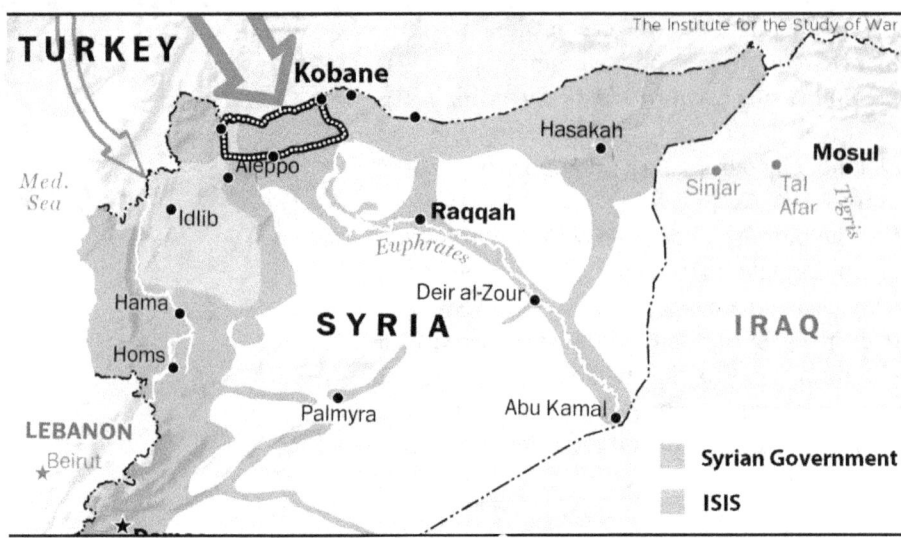

The ISIS terrorists captured the wonderful, beautiful city of Palmyra, which was one of the architectural treasures of the world. They began to loot, and the looted material was sent up through the Kobane gap and marketed in Turkey. Additionally, in Mosul in Iraq, a city of a million or so captured by ISIS troops, they had seized major hospitals and they forced the doctors to do live removal of human body parts which would be packed in ice and shipped again through the Kobane gap and sold on the market through Turkey and also through Saudi Arabia. There is a tremendous amount of money in live body parts, because they could literally select the size. If you have a child, you could get a child's organs. There were various reports of Iraqi doctors who were beheaded for refusing,— they simply refused to open up live children and extract their organs.

But this is the type of trade that our good ally, our NATO ally, Turkey, conducts. Turkey is essentially an organized criminal enterprise. This is how they function, this is how they fund themselves. The President of Turkey, President Erdogan, has now won total control of the Parliament, and they're going to rewrite the Constitution. He has declared that he wants powers similar to those of Adolf Hitler. We are now fighting alongside, in a coalition with, a man who says that he wants the powers of Adolf Hitler.

And so, as we negotiate for peace in Syria today, we have a spider on one side and a scorpion on the other, and those are Turkey and Saudi Arabia, two of the most vile dictatorships in the world. The Turks have a long history of murdering Christians in the Armenian genocide. They're now killing off Kurds within Turkey. The Kurds are about 20 percent of the Turkish population. We have Saudi Arabia, which has *absolutely* no freedom whatsoever. Women are viewed as total property, and there still is slavery that goes on. They officially abolished slavery in 1962, but it still goes on to some extent even to this day.

The Russian Intervention

So those are our grand allies, the ones that we think we should rely on to improve Syria. The Russians, in what can only be described as an absolutely heroic act on the part of President Putin, moved in with a relatively modest military force. They attacked the oil supply, they began driving back the Army of Conquest and shrinking it in this area. They began bombing around Aleppo, the major industrial center of Syria. Everywhere, the rebels, ISIS, and al-Qaeda are falling back on every single front throughout the country.

So, in summary, I would simply ask, what would end this war? If we want this war to end, and it is essential to American vital interests in the Middle East that Syria survive and that the terrorists be defeated, the way to do it is to cut off the TOW anti-tank missiles that we are continuing to send in and that we are allowing the Saudi Arabians and the Turks to send in. We must restore peace to the Middle East. Syria is the key to doing it. When this war ends, this tremendous wave of jihadist activity across the globe will begin to subside.

It's going to be essential that, as it does, we start putting the thumb on Saudi Arabia, which is exporting this Wahhabist *poisonous* breed of Islamic radicalism which causes, literally, thousands of attacks across the globe *monthly,* on a monthly basis! It's a remarkable number! And so, we've got to stop the terrorism, and the place to start is in Syria.

So, thank you very much for listening, and we hope that you enjoy the Schiller conference.

II. The Human Unity of Classical Culture

HELGA ZEPP-LAROUCHE

Change History by Ennobling Man

Dennis Speed: To introduce our opening remarks person, I'd like to quote something that some of you may have heard before, in part, from Percy Shelley's *In Defense of Poetry*:

"But poets, or those who imagine and express this indestructible order, are not only the authors of language and of music, of the dance, and architecture, and statuary, and painting: They are the institutors of laws, and the founders of civil society, and the inventors of the arts of life, and the teachers, who draw into a certain propinquity with the beautiful and the true that partial apprehension of the agencies of the invisible world which is called religion. Hence all original religions are allegorical, or susceptible of allegory, and, like Janus, have a double face of false and true. Poets, according to the circumstances of the age and nation in which they appeared, were called, in the earlier epochs of the world, legislators, or prophets: A poet essentially comprises and unites both these characters. ..."

The Schiller Institute is named after a poet, and all of its actions are intended to be poetic, informed by the principles of poetry and the idea of Classical poetry. The person who took it upon herself to conduct a mission to impart that profound and impassioned idea of poetry to America in particular, and to the world in general, also founded the organization which has convened

EIRNS/Stuart Lewis

Helga Zepp-LaRouche, participating in Panel I of the April 7 Schiller Institute Conference in New York City.

you here today. I'd like Helga LaRouche, founder of the Schiller Institute, to come and give us opening remarks.

Helga Zepp-LaRouche: Confucius wrote many important things about music and the relationship between music and the state. He said, if you want to judge the condition of a country, you should look at its music. Now, by that measurement, I think we in the West are in *deep* trouble.

So that is why the Schiller Institute has given the highest importance to Classical music, and Classical art in general. But in a society which is so divided—in which all the issues are so divisive, and people have so many opinions that you cannot find two people who agree on one point of any given issue—how do you get it back to truth-seeking? And, to seek the truth no matter what you do, *no matter what you do,* if it's music, if it's teaching, if it's science, if it's doing business, people should be truthful. Because only then are they really human beings.

The only areas where truth-seeking is truly possible without the deviation of being opinionated or just taking over the opinion of someone else—the media, your neighbors, whatever—the two areas where it is possible to seek the truth are natural science, because there you can discover principles which are universal, because when you discover them in Germany, they also function in China, or in the United States, so therefore, there is a criterion of truth. And the only other area where this applies fully, is Classical art. Because only in Classical art can you find principles which are as eternal and as truthful as scientific principles.

So the question therefore, is how do we get society

And that is why the beauty in everything, especially in Classical art, is so absolutely crucial, because beauty is an expression of reason. Schiller demands that beauty be defined, not by experience, but by reason. But at the same time, beauty is also manifest naturally in the realm of the senses, and therefore, there is no contradiction between reason and emotions, in beautiful art and other expressions of beauty.

---

back—healed—from the terrible condition in which it is right now?

Educate the Emotions

Well, we have to educate people again to know what beauty is. In Schiller's famous controversy with Kant, Kant said, in the categorical imperative, "you *must.*" "You must be moral, you must act in such a way that you will not violate the rights of someone else...." Schiller was horrified by this, and said, "Poor Kant! He must have had a terrible childhood, because he only wrote for slaves, for servants, and not for beautiful souls." The beautiful soul is one that loves freedom so much, that it does not even want to contemplate a procedure to force itself to be moral: That would mean suppressing something, and true freedom must not suppress.

And that is why the beauty

in everything, especially in Classical art, is so absolutely crucial, because beauty is an expression of reason. Schiller demands that beauty be defined, not by experience, but by reason. But at the same time, beauty is also manifest naturally in the realm of the senses, and therefore, there is no contradiction between reason and emotions, in beautiful art and other expressions of beauty.

Schiller was absolutely convinced that the most important task of his time was to educate the emotions. Because if people are emotionally crippled, so that they have only one faculty or skill, and have neglected all others, or if they have somehow mismanaged their whole life, the only remedy is through the education of the emotions, up to the point where your emotions guide you on the level of reason, so that you can blindly follow whatever your impulse is, because it is never against what reason would command.

Now Schiller called this "aesthetical education." And the way to achieve it is through great Classical art. He had much to say in the beautiful *Aesthetical Letters* as to why *only* great Classical art can bring about the moral improvement and ennoblement of the individual. He was convinced—and it has been my firm *credo* for a very long time—that change in politics cannot come through *anything* but through the ennoblement of the individual. So therefore, let's have some beautiful art, and understand that this is politics on the highest level.

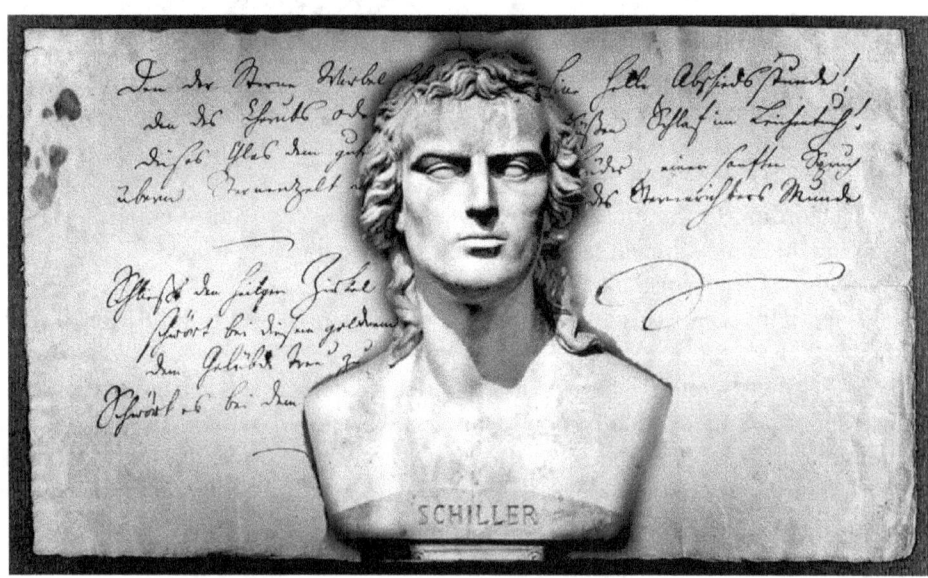

Bust of Friedrich Schiller on a manuscript of the "Ode to Joy".

BEN WANG

The Unity of Calligraphy, Poetry, Painting, and Music in Chinese Art

Dennis Speed: I met our next speaker, although he didn't exactly know that he met me, at the Metropolitan Museum, where he was sharing the lectern with another presenter, an American, who was insisting on presenting, shall we say, a slightly veiled quasi-political agenda; but our speaker was able to gently persuade the audience that, perhaps, there was a deeper function of culture, than a political bludgeon.

Prof. Ben Wang is an author, translator, and senior lecturer in languages and humanities at the China Institute of Columbia University.

EIRNS/Stuart Lewis

Ben Wang, addressing the April 7, 2016 Schiller Institute Conference in New York.

Prof. Ben Wang: Those are hard acts to follow. [laughter] I brought some Chinese tea. I think I should serve each speaker a little bit for five minutes, and then I will start making my much lesser talk, and people will bear with me. As it is, I have to speak right after them, so I feel a little nervous. But I'm sure you will give me a lot of allowance.

We're talking about things old and gone away, but as my favorite writer of England, Muriel Spark says, "The glory of the past is the inspiration for the future." So, although we are talking about something old, I know something new will be born. As Tennessee Williams says, "Violets in the mountains have broken the rocks," which is written on his tombstone. There's always hope. But tonight we talk about the glory of the past.

What I'm going to talk about is called Literati Painting, which is uniquely limited to Chinese culture. Because of the time limitation I will have to read. Usually, I

am given two or three hours. Before I forget, I must thank Miss Lynn Yen and the Foundation for the Revival of Classical Culture, and Dennis, of course, for letting me come, for which I am very grateful. I begged for more time, but after much negotiation, much talk on my side, I got ten minutes more. [laughter] They were going to give me twenty minutes; I said, "it's hardly enough, because I'm a master of digression." So when I do, you must stop me. But seeing how old I am, I know you won't, but I want you to! Just say, "stop," and "go ahead."

Because there are other wonderful,— this is a very rich night! You know, in fact, I'm not trying to kiss up to Miss Yen or the Foundation or Dennis, but I don't remember attending an event like this. In my totally ignorant idea about speeches, about events, I was usually the only speaker, and the topic is usually on poetry, on Literati Painting, on drama, on music, on theater. So to have such a rich program—I mean, the two before, took my breath away! And after the tenor, I just said to myself, "How can I go on talking?" you know? And my voice, I'm under the influence of a cold, but normally, I sound very good—almost as good as him. [laughter] Not quite . . . maybe 60 years ago.

So, what is Literati Painting? It is,— I'm sorry to say, it might be very unfamiliar to a Western ear. It's all these three ingredients: poetry, calligraphy, and painting. Now, as shown on the screen:

Poetry, held in the highest esteem in Chinese culture,

is the most significant of the three components—poetry, calligraphy, and painting—that make up the genre of Literati Painting of China, which was created during the Song Dynasty (960-1280), from the late 10th century until the late 13th century, before the Yuan dynasty. Literati Painting reached its pinnacle with the patronage of one of the first and most eminent Manchurian emperors, Qianlong (1736-1796) of the Qing dynasty (1644-1911).

Now at this juncture, I must make something clear: Long before Literati Painting emerged, China already had 2,000 years of culture and civilization. So why did it take so long for Literati Painting to emerge? Because every literary or artistic genre is like a baby: Chinese Literati Painting is a lovely baby. Where does a lovely baby come from? From a lovely man and a lovely woman. And the two of them, they have to be grown up in order to be in union, to be married and to have the child. Because Literati Painting consists of three ingredients: poetry, calligraphy, and painting. So it took the Chinese almost 2,000 years for the three forms to mature, for poetry to mature, for calligraphy and painting to mature, and then, the three in union, they create— the three of them—a grand *ménage à trois*. They create this lovely baby that is called Literati Painting. That's why it took so long!

There Is Everything In It

During the period between 1100 and 500 B.C., the first collection of 300 poems appears on the scene, which is the earliest human poetry ever in world history, which is called *Book of Songs*, as it is translated by Arthur Waley. It still makes very good reading. Well, wonderful literature doesn't die, quite like an old soldier, it doesn't die. And so, if you find a copy of the *Book of Songs*, by all means, read it.

Painting didn't start until about 300 B.C. And calligraphy matured; it started as oral language and then seal types, and finally, the current writing. And speaking of which, we must go back to the special, unique quality of the Chinese language. All languages in the world are unique. But for something nonpareil, Chinese language is that: quite nonpareil, in that spoken Chinese is music, and written Chinese is painting. That's why in Literati Painting, there is everything. There are tones, which actually are music, and there is poetry, and there is calligraphy, and there is painting. Actually, painting serves as the supplementary aspect to this genre.

So, let's go on.

Fusing poetic profundity, calligraphy and tonal splendor, and painting of poignancy, Literati Painting blooms in an enchanted garden of literature, music, and fine art—a garden that has been treasured by the Chinese and the world for the past one thousand years.

This lecture focuses on two timeless works by Qi Baishi.

There have been hundreds or thousands of works, but I have selected only two. If you want to know why, take it up with Lynn Yen and the Foundation. I had 200 prepared; I can speak of only two. [laughter] I'm just joking, feebly. Someone says, "Oh, always blaming someone else."

Qi Baishi—please remember this name. He is the last giant of Literati Painting. I often say, with his demise, with his death, came also the death of Literati Painting: Because no one can even write poetry, can even write Classical poetry, in Chinese any more. He is the towering master of Literati Painting of the Twentieth Century. An in-depth study of the nuances and underlying imageries and the exquisite musicality of his poems, as well as the refinement and beauty of his calligraphy and paintings, will enable us all to heighten the pleasure of appreciating Chinese culture.

About Qi Baishi (1864-1959). Qi Baishi's world of art transforms the commonplace of life into poetic romanticism. Born of a peasant and bucolic origin, Qi Baishi produced works which are filled with a sense of closeness to the land, which is well captured in his extraordinarily poignant depiction of shrimp, fish, wildflowers, and birds, among other seemingly inconsequential objects of nature. Added into those paintings are his poems and calligraphy, both of which are marked by an unrestrained bravura and spirit.

Qi Baishi's acute sense for the colorfulness of nature, employed to reflect love, life, memory, and the transitoriness of beauty and art, affords him the surest passport to immortality.

Now let's look at the two works by him, which I would say is the main course of this feast.

This (**Figure 1**) is a painting of morning-glories, and this grasshopper is brown, light brown, which means it's very old; because young grasshoppers are very green. Only when they become old (like myself), does the color fade until finally they become whitish. So this grasshopper is not dark; I mean, grasshoppers are never dark, when they are very young they're green, but this one is light brown. And he morning-glories are deep purple, between purple and burgundy red. This is the morning-glory. So this is the painting.

FIGURE 1

Where Does the Meaning Lie?

The great Chinese artists, they walk a thin line between likeness and unlikeness. To have their paintings look exactly like the real thing, would be too much, too close to realism. They must transcend realism and reach magical illusionism. So this is between likeness and unlikeness, between realism and magical illusionism. So, the grasshopper is coming out of the bushes of the morning-glories. We all know that morning-glories only open in the morning, and when the Sun almost reaches the middle of the sky,— but when we're approaching noon, all the morning-glories wither.

And pay attention to where he is walking to. He is lowering his head toward the west. Chinese culture is heavily influenced by Indian art; so before, when I was listening to Tagore's poem, although I don't understand Bengali, yet I could be moved: That's what poetry and beauty can do, even if you don't understand the language. For instance, when we listen to opera, I don't really, always, understand what's being sung, but I can appreciate the music.

So to the Chinese, the west is Nirvana. We call it the World of Extreme Happiness,— so that means the grasshopper is old, and he has experienced all his happy and healthy golden days; now he's walking toward the west, to Nirvana,— to put it plainly, to death.

And there are two lines of poetry. These are heptasyllabic lines.

So these are two heptasyllabic poetic lines, a poetic couplet. In Chinese the most popular poetic styles are either pentasyllabic or heptasyllabic, meaning five characters per line, or seven characters per line. The Chinese language is a monosyllabic language: Every character, every word-character has only one syllable, so when I say, "heptasyllabic," that means seven characters per line.

So you look at this painting, you feel—wow!—it's a mixture of tenderness, exquisiteness, and something bravura, because of the brushwork. Yet, what is important does not lie in the picture or in the grasshopper or in the morning-glory, but they are all serving as supplementary to the poem.

So he put down these two lines. What exactly does it mean, "Use you Pull Cattle (in capital letters) Magpie Bridge (capital letters) pass"? Then, "Then two temple but no frost"? What does that mean? Maybe that's what makes the non-Chinese, the Westerners, ask, What are you saying? Are you speaking Chinese? [laughter] You know? Because it defies understanding, unless you understand Chinese—except this is Classical Chinese.

So the artist is addressing directly to,— he is the grasshopper. The grasshopper has taken the persona of the poet. So he has just come out of this. So he is talking to the morning-glory. He says, "I have once used you, I have employed you. You are the one who helped me, you are the Pull Cattle flower." Morning-glory in Chinese is called "Pull Cattle." Why do you think the Chinese would call the morning-glory "Pull Cattle?" Because morning-glory only blooms, only opens when the Sun is up, when it's the crack of dawn it starts to open. So it's time for the Chinese farmers to pull the cattle, to pull the water buffalo out to work the field. So the Chinese said, "Oh, these flowers, they should be called, 'Pull Cattle' or call for cattle to wake up and help us, drag us to work on the land." So in Chinese—that's why it's in capital letters—"Pull Cattle" is the Chinese name for morning-glory.

So, once upon a time, I used you, my dear Pull Cattle flowers. And you have helped me pass the Magpie Bridge.

Now, there's another folksy and also literary allusion to this. And the magpie is connected with a very sad Chinese story which is not unlike Romeo and Juliet. It's about a thwarted pair of star-crossed lovers. They can meet only once a year, and the woman is a celestial being, so she's a weaving-woman in the celestial palace; she comes down to the Earth, she meets this shepherd boy. He tends to cattle, so he is a cowherd, the Chinese answer to a cowboy. So they fall in love, but she is a celestial being, so she is called back by the king of the celestial palace,— so they can never meet again. One old buffalo takes pity on them, and when he dies he says to the shepherd boy, "you've been so sweet to me, and I like that girl, the celestial being that you married who has gone back to the celestial palace. So after I die, you cut my hide and every year, on the seventh day of the seventh lunar month, you wrap my hide around you, then you can fly. So I will help you to fly into the sky to meet with your lover."

What Is It About?

And in the meantime all the magpies, they took pity on these two thwarted and star-crossed lovers, so in the firmament, in the Milky Way, there is a river which is called Silvery River, and the magpies, in flocks, lay in the river—the river is not that deep. So that allowed the shepherd boy to walk on their bodies to go across the bridge to meet his loved one.

So this is the story. So he said, "My dear morning-glory, once I used you to cross the Magpie Bridge. But alas, at that time, the two temples on my head ..." this temple is not a Buddhist temple; it is this temple [points to his head], the two sides. That's where the white hair, like my hair, first grows. It usually starts with the temples.

"But at that time, the two temples of mine, there was no frost on them." To the Chinese why did hair turn white? Obviously Heaven has sent some frost onto your hair, so your hair turns white.

So this is referring to the white hair.

What is this painting all about? It is the remembrance of lost love, of lost happiness, and golden, healthier days, everything that is lost,— but once upon a time, there was love, there was beauty, so it's worth remembering. So instead of crying, or any lamentation, or any lugubrious message to feel sad-

denned by this remembrance, the artist uses this very discreet way of expressing what is on his mind. Remember, all great artists can *never* forget that human beings are the basic subject of all art. So out of poetic imagination and great compassion, they spin loving, poignant, and luminous works. This great Chinese master of painting, calligraphy, and poetry is no exception; here is this seemingly non-human composition, referring to everything in the human mind about remembrance.

And now quickly we come to the finale. This one is one of Qi Baishi's signature pieces and masterpieces, I would say. In 1948, right after the Sino-Japanese War, when China suffered from unprecedented invasion and the cruelty of a savage war of eight years, it was immediately followed by a civil war between the Communists and the Nationalists. Full of painful sentiments and emotions about what is happening around him, Qi Baishi, being an artist only—he's no politician, no great military man—what can he do about the bad times that he was living in, era after era, decade after decade?

So, in desperation and in sadness, he composed this painting (**Figure 2**). And you see two chicks, and he deliberately leaves out the tail of this chick [on the left], so the composition of this painting is a little more interesting. It's less pedantic, I would say.

And also, do you see how they stare at each other? And this is all brushwork. And here is the earthworm they're fighting over. And so, is he really painting two chicks for us, for the viewer to enjoy it? No. Because the heart of the matter is here: Now these four characters are the heart of the matter. And these two characters were his signature. His literary sobriquet was "white stone." So this is "white" and "stone." To the Chinese, white represents purity and rock represents perseverance and fortitude.

So these four characters are *ta ri hu xiang*; this character *ta* in modern Chinese means "he." But in Classical Chinese, and it derives from Classical Chinese, it means "the other," "some other." "Some other day": this (*ri*) is "day"; the picture is "the Sun is rising." This comes from the Sun. Every Chi-

FIGURE 2

nese character is derived from a picture, so "Sun" represents a day. So "some other day." Then *xiang* originally showed a Chinese farmer's eye set on a tree, which means he is very fascinated by the tree. He wants to know the age of the tree, what kind of tree it is, whether or not it should be used as firewood or in the lumberyard. So *xiang* came to mean "to each other" or "with each other" or a mutual relationship. So my translation is "to-each-other." *Hu* is call out; the mouth is the radical, so this is to call out, "hellooo!" And how does he express this "hellooo," the echo? By moving this stroke *all* the way around like this. Normally when you write this stroke, you just go up to here, you go up a little bit. But yet, he goes all the way around.

So, in 1948, when the Civil War was going on, he was heartbroken! So he was saying, "Communist Nationalist or Nationalist Communist, now you're fighting for the land of China. But remember, we're all Chinese. One day, I hope—you're both chicks now—some day, when there is a stormy day, or blizzard, or rainy day, but you will grow up to be a big rooster, and so will I. We are brothers, we're siblings, we grew up together. Now we are very ignorant, we're small babies, we fight over an earthworm. But some day, when we grow up, no matter

what the day is, if you call from the neighboring village two miles away, I will hear you, I will call. I will say, "Hey, Brother, are you still there?" And so the other rooster will say, "Yes, I'm still here, and I wish you well." So we'll still be siblings. We will remain siblings.

This is the great artist's *hope*, his compassion, his passion, his wish for the two parties that were in a bloody war, to come to a peace. Or, maybe not in his lifetime, but one day, when they grow up. And now, for sure, the President of Taiwan has gone to meet with the President of People's Republic of China, and I think Qi Baishi's dream has come true.

So this is seemingly,— he uses painting, art, to talk about politics, to talk about war, to talk about human fights as strife, the disgusting war, the bloody war; but he uses beauty and art and poetry.

I know I have run more than 35 minutes, so I really must quickly come to an end. I will say something else, that my favorite Tennessee Williams, the greatest poet-playwright of America in my mind, in my opinion, says, "what implements have we, what words, images, colors, music, scratches upon our caves of solitude?" I think Qi Baishi, if he had heard these words, would have been in total agreement with Williams. Thank you very much.

CARMELA ALTAMURA

Verdi's Operas and Italy's *Risorgimento* Movement

Dennis Speed: For about a year, members of the Schiller Institute have been involved in the creation of city-wide choruses, and we've done some performances of the Handel *Messiah;* we've done two in Brooklyn and one in Manhattan. But in the course of work that we were doing, one of the members of the Schiller Institute, Mr. Lyndon LaRouche, kept talking about what he called "the Italian principle." He said that if you really want to do this right, you've got to assert the "Italian principle," the placement of the voice, the proper placement of the voice. And when I met the next speaker, without any of that being said to her, this was what she was simply talking about. She has known this; this isn't anything new to her.

Now the reason this becomes very important is that Classical culture, when performed properly, is the most powerful weapon for oppressed people in the world. To speak on the topic, "Verdi's Operas and Italy's *Risorgimento* Movement," I'm pleased to welcome to the stage Carmela Altamura, soprano and vocal instructor, founder and director of Inter-Cities Performing Arts and of the Altamura/Caruso International Voice Competition.

Carmela Altamura: Ladies, Friends, what a joy! The energy in this room is enough to transform the world. Congratulations to all of you for having taken time, love, passion to create something that will last forever. Because it is *love* that moves all of your genius. It is love! The whole world moves on love.

EIRNS/Stuart Lewis

Carmela Altamura

The founders, Mr. and Mrs. LaRouche, are to be venerated, congratulated, and all of the guests, the speakers, the performers—and you, all of you are accomplished, all of you are geniuses.

And so, I'll tell you a few words now. In 1987, the idea came to me, after having worked for 14 years in a school for the community, for dispossessed, and for the expatriates of the communist world. Since the population began to change and the Cubans moved to Florida, I thought it was time to close the school and create a company called Inter-Cities Performing Arts, Inc. It became a compulsion, became a drive for me to create something, to improve ethnic, social, professional, and cultural relations in the world, through the arts. And so two programs were born out of that: The Altamura/Caruso International Voice Competition, and the school, the Altamura Center for the Arts, where the winners of these competitions would have the opportunity to have advanced studies and meet and encounter the real masters who would transmit the wisdom—not written—by voice; this is the tradition of the *bel canto.*

You cannot write everything down anyway. The word, unless it's married to music, has its own limitations.

I made a few innovations that caused a little stir in the world. I took away the age limit. That came like an atomic bomb in the cultural world. "What on Earth is this lady doing! What is she talking about?" Well, there was a need to do that, because very important voices which are needed for the Verdi, and Puccini and Wagner repertoire, mature later—psychologically, physically, hormonally—and I saw that need.

What happened after that—even though I took a little abuse, but I have thick skin—we discovered great, great voices, which today are performing in the major, prestigious theaters of the world, such as the bassi, the dramatic sopranos, and mezzosopranos, the contralti, and the coloratura, you know.

This is why I feel attached to Verdi, because of this impact. I took the winners to Milano, to the home for retired artists, which Verdi founded. He was a *great* humanitarian and philanthropist. He founded hospitals, he founded this rest home, and there, my singers were immediately booked for La Scala to do *Attila.* You know, *Attila* requires a very heavy voice.

My competition took its place in the world. I raised the bar, and I chose Giulietta Simionato; I don't know if any of you know her, but she was the premiere mezzosoprano at that time in the world. In order to raise the bar right away, my first competition took place at the Lincoln Center. And I had *nerve*—I was nervy—and I wrote to the United States Congress. I said: "If La Scala gets a letter from the United States Congress, maybe they will listen." And so, they let her go, and she came to the United States and became my first president of this competition.

Giuseppe Verdi: The Voice of Italy

And of course, I am very enamored—ever since I was a little girl—of Verdi. I remember my father taking me to Palermo; I was only six. I saw *Rigoletto,* which frightened me; the hunchback frightened me terribly, but when Gilda came out, I immediately memorized "Tutte le feste al tempio." And in my hometown, they put me on a little tobacco box, and I would sing. Of course, I would get lots of candy, so I sang "Tutte le feste al tempio" from one corner of the town to the other end. And then, at the age of eight, after the world war, I came to the United States, and on that ship they discovered me.

But anyway, I'm not here to talk about myself, I'm here to talk about Verdi and the *Risorgimento.* Verdi is the voice of Italy. He's the *unifying* voice of Italy. When Verdi was born in 1813, the land was under French rule; it would only last another year, because then Napoleon was defeated. And little Verdi, being a child of destiny—I should tell you this little story, because I think that men of destiny are born under a special star, especially if they are to do something transformative for the world.

He was barely a week old, and the Austrians invaded, to push out the French. They hired the Cossacks: nothing new under the Sun—to speak about ISIS, forget about it. They were worse! So the priest said to the poor women, "Go into the church, there you will be safe." So all the women and the babies went to the church. And Luigia Uttini, which was the name of Giuseppe Verdi's mommy, went also, with the child in her arms, but she decided not to stay in the church; she decided to go the sacristy, and from the sacristy she saw the stairs going to the belfry. She climbed the stairs all the way up to the belfry; the child never cried. In the morning, when the Sun came up, there was complete silence. She went down the steps. She thought by now, everybody's gone. And when she came down, she saw, everyone had been slaughtered. Only little Verdi and she were alive.

Now, if you go there today, to that church, there is a plaque, that tells you that this is a very special place.

At the age of three, he was studying Latin, math, Italian. Imagine! Now, the father, realizing that this child was highly musical, went out, and on his back, carried this little piano—you know, it was no bigger than me; now it's at La Scala, on permanent display. And he brought it to the child. And the child began, and he suddenly started to make little melodies, and with the left hand—by now he was six. And the people in the tavern said "doesn't this child ever stop playing?" "No! He's got this passion for the music!"

And little Verdi, at the age of eight, was deputizing for his teacher, who was ill at that time; he took his place in church, to take care of all the church functions, and weddings and funerals. Can you imagine that? And he took his stipend, and he brought it to his parents. Try to find that today.

He helped his mother gather the mulberry leaves; she produced the silk worms, and the poor child, he would go with his big basket on his back, and bring all these leaves to his mother, trip after trip after trip.

So these are the little stories.

Now, they take Verdi for advanced studies in Milano. But before he goes to Milano, he goes to Busseto and Mr. Barezzi, a prominent businessman, decides to take him under his wing. It was evident that this child was extraordinary, so they sent him to the Conservatory. And he auditions: They did not accept him.

Verdi was heartbroken. And so was Mr. Barezzi. But they would not give up because they knew this was political. The judges said, "His hand does not sit properly on the piano, and his compositions, maybe if he studies some counterpoint, someday he might become a veritable composer." "Veritable?" He wrote 27 operas. He never made it to the Conservatory. So I should tell the students, never get discouraged. Just work, work, work, work, and persistence, and perseverance, that's the gift.

And Verdi gets married to Barezzi's daughter, who was a soprano. Her name was Margherita, a beautiful girl, very holy. They have a little girl, Virginia, who twelve months later dies. They try again and have a little boy, Icilio. Eighteen months later, he dies. Discouraged, disappointed, and depressed, they go back to Milano looking for work. His wife Margherita sells even her jewelry; he doesn't know about it. She sells everything, and Verdi never knew that. Then she falls ill, and she dies.

National Gallery of Modern Art/Giuseppe Verdi by Giovanni Boldini
Giuseppe Verdi (1813-1901)

'Va Pensiero'

Before this happened, he meets a soprano by the name of Giuseppina Strepponi, a very famous star at La Scala. And Giuseppina recognized this great talent, and she goes to Merelli who was the general manager of La Scala, and he believes her, and so he gives Verdi a commission for the first opera, *Oberto, Conte di San Bonifacio*. Verdi had it in his blood. So this was 1840. He had it in his blood.

He is commissioned for 14 operas; not bad for a young composer. But, when his wife dies, Verdi puts down the pen, and says, "No more. I will not write another note." And dejected, depressed, sorrowful, and sick to the core of his heart, he moves into third floor loft apartment, cold flat, and he finds some chestnuts, and that's all he had.

But then there is destiny. It happens that the general manager of La Scala has a libretto in his hands, but that his chosen composer refused to do it. So he sends someone to fetch Verdi, who does not want to go at first. Some stories say it was Giuseppina, and others say that he sent someone else. But Verdi did go. The general manager told him that he had a beautiful script, "it is wonderful!" It's about the exiled Jews, and Verdi says, "So what?" "No, this is very important, I want you to read it."

"I told you, I will not write another note."

"Listen to me, this is good. Go!" He puts it under his arm, shoves him out the door, and Verdi, with the libretto under his arm, goes home. He throws the libretto angrily on the nearby table. Do you know where it opened? Verdi looks, and he reads, "Fly, thought, on golden wings," the translation of "Va pensiero, sull'ali dorate."

Verdi closes it again—"No! No, no, no, no!" and he goes to bed. After fifteen minutes, he gets up again … what? What was that? And he reads it again. Hmm, well, I suppose I could write a few notes. He goes to the piano, and he puts down a few notes. And he writes the melody, renowned all over the world, "Va pensiero, sull'ali dorate." He takes it back to La Scala, and about a year later, the opera is being produced, and Donizetti—do you know Donizetti?—he was in the theater at the time; it was a Thursday. And a mechanic said to him, "Listen, go. You've seen the rehearsal already." He said, "No, no, I'm staying here." When it was time to perform the "Va, pensiero," all the people that worked in opera house, they froze! And on Sunday, they performed the opera [*Nabucco*]. And from being an unknown,— soon every little barrel organ in Milano was playing the melodies. All the sauces were "alla Verdi," the hats were "alla Verdi," the clothes were "alla Verdi," and his career began.

Verdi said, "I never had peace after that." All I did was work like a dog. He never saw the sunlight.

The woman who really helped him though, was the Giuseppina Strepponi, with whom he lived for 10 years.

Unifying Italy Through Beauty

Now as for the *Risorgimento*, the movement that unified Italy, Verdi was in communication with Mazzini and Garibaldi, and Alessandro Manzoni, who at this time had written the novel, *I Promessi Sposi* (The Betrothed), and had given Italy its language! And so every opera that Verdi wrote after that—*I Lombardi alla Prima Crocciata* (The Lombards on the First Crusade), *Giovanna d'Arco* (Joan of Arc)—every opera was written on the subject of the *tyranny* of the reigning house.

Italy becomes one. Italy becomes unified, and in 1870, we now have a country called Italy.

Verdi's name, when he was baptized, was Giuseppe Fortunino Franceso Verdi. And through him the country was unified, the Italians were unified, and he loved everyone who had helped him.

But, Ladies and Gentlemen, there is something I want to read to you tonight, and I want to leave you with this story. Tonight, everyone spoke about nature, about unity, about oneness. There is one in Italy who happens to be the patron saint of Italy; it is St. Francis of Assisi. We are in the middle of the Thirteenth Century. These words are religious, but the wisdom is the same for every religion. But they go *beyond* religion, they go to the core of truth, and truth is not learned, Ladies and Gentlemen, truth is revealed, and it is revealed only to those with a pure heart.

This is called the "Prayer of St. Francis":

"Lord, make me an instrument of thy peace.
Where there is hatred, let me sow love;
Where there is injury, pardon;
Where there is doubt, faith;
Where there is despair, hope;
Where there is darkness, light;
Where there is sadness, joy.
O divine Master, grant that I may not so much seek
To be consoled as to console,
To be understood as to understand,
To be loved as to love;
For it is in giving that we receive;
It is in pardoning that we are pardoned;
It is in dying to self that we are born to eternal life."

This is the message of oneness: If we all take a little responsibility, each one of us, the world will be transformed. It is time, or it is too late.

CONDUCTOR ANTHONY MORSS

What Is Classical Culture?

Anthony Morss spoke at the April 7 Schiller Institute conference, representing the Foundation for the Revival of Classical Culture.

Friedrich Schiller, newly appointed professor of history at Jena University, chose as the topic for his inaugural lecture, "What is—and to what end do we study—Universal History?" My topic this evening is "What is—and to what end do we study—Classical Culture?"

Classical Culture has three meanings:

(1) Of or pertaining to the culture of ancient Greece and Rome

(2) Any works of art which by their beauty and shapeliness and perfect proportions remind us of that classical heritage

(3) Any art so conspicuously magnificent that it sets its own standard for all future judgment.

Rules of thumb for assessing any work of art are well known and essentially universally accepted: The principle of unity in diversity, and the idea that in art of the highest quality, nothing can be added and nothing taken away without diminishing the value of the work.

Greek aesthetics also pointed out that the art work's size must be proportioned to our ability to perceive, that is, not so small that we cannot perceive the component parts, and not so large that we cannot cognize the totality of it. These last points are just common sense.

Fundamental to the value of the art is that it must be experienced as organic, by which I mean that it must mimic convincingly the organization and functioning of a large, complex organism like a human being, comprising many different organs and support systems like

EIRNS/Stuart Lewis
Conductor Anthony Morss addressed the question, What is Classical Culture?

the blood, the lymph, the electrochemical activity in the brain—all with the purpose of allowing the person to fulfill his choice of projects.

This system can be called a manifold, and all of us are biological manifolds. But there are mechanical manifolds as well, such as an automobile engine with many ancillary systems all connected to, and empowering, the central motor. On the simplest level, a pipe with several transverse openings is a manifold.

These intricately interconnected systems of supportive activity mirror the organization of the outside world as revealed by science. The fundamental presupposition of all scientific activity, as defined by Lyndon LaRouche, is that the organizing principles of the universe are coherent with the rational structure of the human brain. That is, we know the universe is governed by scientific laws, some of which we have discovered and many we have not. If we didn't think there were many scientific laws waiting to be discovered, we wouldn't go looking for them, which is what scientists spend their lives doing. Mr. LaRouche's statement is so self-evidently true that it almost amounts to a tautology, yet the words strike one with the force of brilliance.

So we have determined that works of art, inanimate objects as they are, must display the characteristics of complex living organisms, with all their intricate cat's cradle of inner relationships. How this can work out in practical terms is illustrated by a famous, long conversation between Jan Sibelius and Gustav Mahler, who on their first meeting took a long walk together and described their artistic ideals. Both composers had written several symphonies and Mahler was, of course, one of the two most famous conductors in the world, the other being Arthur Nikisch.

Sibelius said that what he most admired about symphonic composition was that one started with a very limited amount of thematic material and evolved all the rest of the work from it. Mahler demurred, saying, "No, no, it must be like the whole world—it must embrace everything!" (*Nein, nein, es muss wie die Welt—es muss alles unfassen!*) Sibelius wanted an organic development, while Mahler wanted to throw even the traditional kitchen sink into the brew—formally undisciplined.

At the end of the walk, Mahler graciously asked Sibelius which of his symphonies he would like Mahler to conduct. Astonishingly, especially considering how famous and influential Mahler was, Sibelius replied, "none of them." He couldn't imagine Mahler could understand what the Sibelius symphonies were trying to say.

Artists' skill in imitating (one might almost say "counterfeiting") nature is essential. There was a classical Greek painter named Appelles of whom it was recounted that he painted a bunch of grapes so realistically that two birds flew into the room and started pecking at the grapes, only to be vexed, as our grandparents used to say, that lunch was not really offered!

But perfect natural copies of objects are not what we demand of painters. Photography will accomplish that. What we require is that painters see and understand and show us beautiful aspects of objects or people that we would not have been able to perceive with our own eyes.

The Breakthroughs We Want

One of my favorite painters in this regard is the venerated Northern Sung Chinese landscape painter Fan Kuan (circa 1000 A.D.) Fan Kuan developed such convincing different brushstrokes to evoke all the different forms of vegetation, branches, pine needles, and such that the commentators ascribed to him the intense creativity of nature itself. Yet look at his masterpiece, "Travelers among Mountains and Streams." You can see why the Chinese word for a landscape painting is "mountain-water picture." In this case the grand mountain is not only painted realistically, as any photograph of that district's topography will show, but the whole

scene is vibrating with mysterious power, pointing toward a profoundly spiritual view of nature. Here painting has surpassed personality and connected with something much grander.

Now, what does the Foundation for the Revival of Classical Culture hope to achieve by studying and performing the great works of organic art? More symphonies just like those of Beethoven and Brahms? No, that is not possible because those works, while the results of highly personal individuality, were nonetheless products of the cultural matrix and atmosphere of their time. To write a new Pastoral Symphony like Beethoven's would be to produce a lifeless, artificial creation. What we are trying for by studying the great works of the past is to be inspired by them to produce something equally organic and alive for our own time.

There is a major historical precedent for this, in the creation of opera in Italy at the very end of the Sixteenth Century. For 30 years a society of poets, musicians, singers, and gentlemen scholars, under the direction of Count Bardi in Florence, had been studying intensely how they might revive ancient Greek drama. Their reading showed them that the plays were at least partly sung and danced, or partially declaimed with music in the background, just as the Homeric sagas had been either sung or declaimed while accompanied by the lyre for centuries in ancient times.

For the dance steps they could get some ideas from vase paintings. Regarding the music they were blocked. There are only about 40 remnants of Ancient Greek music and only one complete sentence with that music. And these gentlemen scholars of the Florentine Camerata (or Confraternity) couldn't read the music's clef at all and so couldn't make any use of the surviving fragments—which, to my mind, turned out to be a great advantage. Ancient Greek music—all unisons or octaves and no harmony whatever—was distinctly inferior to Europe's own repertory of polyphonic masterpieces of the High Renaissance. So the music trying to re-create Greek drama began with a highly developed musical language, but instead of contrapuntal settings for many voices singing together, the emphasis was on the alternating voices of characters in the drama (though there also were five-voiced madrigals for the Greek choruses).

Thus, aiming for the faithful reproduction of Ancient Greek drama, these gentlemen scholars produced something quite different but equally great—the first operas! That is the kind of breakthrough we in the Foundation are looking for.

SHRUTI SEN SINGS TAGORE

'Then Walk Alone'

On behalf of Dr. Jayaramanji, an Indian poet, scholar, and founder of the New York Branch of Bharatiya Vidya Bhavan (Institute of Indian Culture), New York Branch, who was unable to attend, Avneet Thapar read his greetings. She then spoke about the great Indian poet Rabindranath Tagore, the revolutionary poet and political resistance leader against the British colonial masters of India. She introduced vocalist Shruti Sen, who sang a classical Indian setting of Tagore's famous poem, "Ekla Chalo Re," written in Bengali (1905).

EIRNS/Stuart Lewis
Shruti Sen

The message from Dr. Panchapakesa Jayaraman:

Cultural Unity Needed for Creating Peace in the World Community

My prayerful message for this dialogue of civilizations is as follows:

The Indian wise men—Sages—have given us numerous instructions for creating classical cultural unity within us.

The following Hymn—Mantra from one of the first and foremost Indian scriptures, Yajurveda—is one among them. Can we not easily follow this principle for creating Peace within us?

> May all beings look on me with the eye of a friend!
> May I look on all beings with the eye of a friend!
> May we look on one another with the eye of a friend!

Another mantra says: May all directions be my friends!

The above should be the basis for building a world-land with all-round unity and peace.

The poem by Rabindranath Tagore, in his own translation:

Ekla Chalo Re

If they answer not to your call, walk alone
If they are afraid and cower mutely facing the wall,
O thou unlucky one,
Open your mind and speak out alone.
If they turn away, and desert you when crossing the
    wilderness,
O thou unlucky one,
Trample the thorns under thy tread,
And along the blood-lined track, travel alone.
If they shut doors and do not hold up the light when
    the night is troubled with storm,
O thou unlucky one,
With the thunder flame of pain ignite your own heart,
And let it burn alone.

Public domain
Rabindranath Tagore (1861-1941), at right, with Jawaharlal Nehru in 1940.

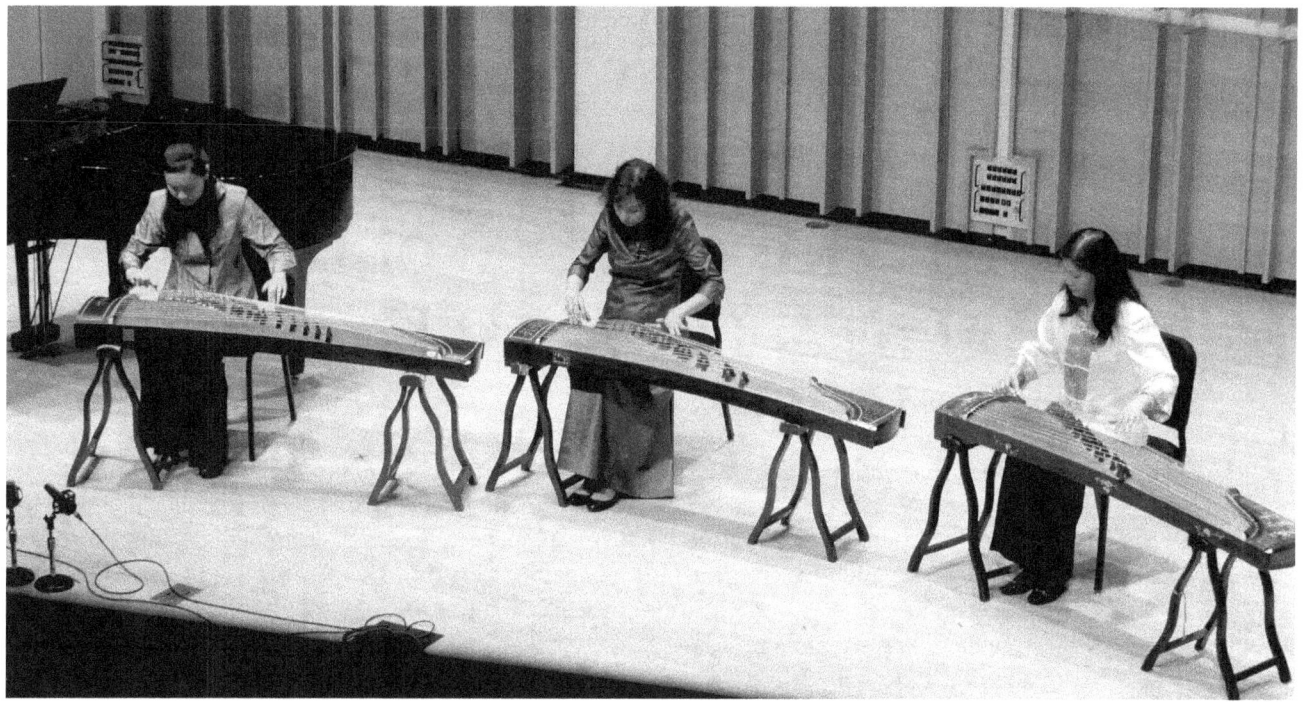

Changyuan Wang, Courtney Hui-Hong Chen, and Zhihui Chen perform on the Chinese Zheng.

Musical Performances During the Panel

Jose Heredia, tenor, **Robert Wilson**, piano

    "Questo o Quella," and "La donna è mobile" from *Rigoletto* by
Giuseppe Verdi

Performance on the Chinese Zheng by **Changyuan Wang**, **Courtney
Hui-Hong Chen**, and **Zhihui Chen**

    "High Mountains and Flowing Streams," music from Zhejiang, arranged
by Xinzhi Wang

    "Battling the Typhoon," by Changyuan Wang

Rachel Hippert, soprano, **Robert Wilson**, piano

    "Willow Song" and "Ave Maria" from *Othello* by Verdi

John Sigerson, tenor, **Yegor Shevtsov**, piano

    Dichterliebe, song cycle by Robert Schumann

'Convey the Importance of the Individual as a Creative Force!'

This is an edited transcript of Lyndon LaRouche's April 9, 2016 Dialogue with the Manhattan Project.

Dennis Speed: We had a conference a couple of days ago which *began* the process which we are going to now *amplify* here and deepen here.

Those of you who were there know that there was a very lively second session. Mr. LaRouche was able, in his capacity as "Dialoguer in Chief," to give some people a lesson in what it means to actually try to think about asking questions. So, Lyn, I'd like to first ask you if there's anything you'd like to say at the beginning, and otherwise we'll start the questions.

Lyndon LaRouche: I would say, simply, that there was a confusion there which was resolved, I think, in the process of presentation, to recognize exactly what the principles are, on which the human voice and mind are capable of understanding each other. I think that's the key mission, is to get a recognition among people of what the truths are, as opposed to some of the jazzed up work, which does not actually amount to anything, in terms of art.

Speed: Maybe we'll have a few questions in that regard. So let's go right to questions. Let's take our first question.

Question: Good afternoon! This is Jessica from Brooklyn, New York. I want to start by talking a little bit about what people have said to me about the conference, and how I've thought about the conference in response.

It was the question and answer period that really stuck out in my mind. After a barrage of statements and non questions from the audience, Kesha Rogers said something that I actually wrote down, and I'm going to repeat it right now: "It's not all these little issues, it's not all this stuff you're talking about—climate change over here (which is ridiculous), and all these other things—that is important; what really is important, is

that this is the threat to your humanity." That's what this was about: the threat to our humanity.

In thinking about that, the entire thing came together to me as "peace through development." I think one of our *EIR* pamphlets said, "Development Is the New Name for Peace," so the "peace through development" idea is there. I want the American people to respond in that way. How do we get the American people to respond to the idea that the Silk Road, and all these other concepts such as the space program represent peace through development? I'd like you to comment on that for us, please.

LaRouche: Okay. The crucial thing that I ran into, in the discussion process, where people were quarreling around this, and arguing this and arguing that, and I simply said, "No!" Because there are certain principles which do define the function of a human being, the true function of a true human being. That's what you have to go for. You have to find out what the truth is and understand why it is the proper instruction to mankind, for the future of mankind.

The problems that arose in some people's minds, were they wanted to bring in all kinds of explanations, other than the name of "human." Our point is that everything is based on the "principle of human," and that principle of human has to be defined correctly, as being the intention to bring mankind to a higher level of achievement for the future of mankind, and that that is the most important issue.

Question: At the conference, there was one thing that you said that really stuck with me, and I'll paraphrase. You said something like, "Science is the process of moving what's in the mind, into physical reality." So, my question is, how do you define what science actually is? And then how can we think more scientifically in the way that Einstein, or a Kepler, or you do?

LaRouche: Well, there's a certain principle there, which can be described summarily, but I don't like to describe it summarily, because it's much more complicated than that. The point is, we all are able, if we wish to—*if* we wish to—to recognize what the meaning of human life is, and people will know it, recognize it, from themselves. People who have any sensitivity at all will recognize this. This is something which is for man, by man, and for the future of mankind. Those principles, which I quoted during the course of that argument there, are the universal principles, as far as I know. These are the principles on which the foundation of mankind's understanding of himself depends. Once they recognize this, they have no choice but to recognize the truth.

Question: Hello, Lyn. My name is A—, from Montreal, Canada. I've been following what this organization's been doing for about a year now. How can we, as organizers when we go out and organize, stick to a certain tradition of beauty, and convey beauty while still trying to expose the ugliness within the culture?

How can we expose the ugliness within the culture, without falling into the ugliness within language? And how can we use certain language that respects the tradition of beauty and exposing beauty through truth?

LaRouche: Simply, you have to understand: You say, "What is Satanic?" Just ask the question, "What is actually Satanic in the common practice of mankind?" You say, "Acts of cruelty against other people." Cheating. Lying. And so forth, as opposed to the simple idea of the desire to *fulfill* something which makes one's life *have meaning* for the future of mankind. That means: What is the progress that we can contribute as individuals, toward the progress of mankind? This is the basis on which different nations, or nationalities, can come together with a common intention; is to get that common intention which creates the success of the human species among *all* participants in human perception. Every nation, every nationality, has a requirement to find in itself something which is truly universal to mankind.

Question: Hi. Thank you for having us here. My

Franklin Roosevelt "was one of the greatest thinkers in the History of the United States" for what he contributed to reconstructing the United States to lift the citizens out of total despair. Here, he visits Chickamauga Dam in Georgia, the fourth of the TVA's main river projects, begun Jan. 13, 1936.

question is: Why, or why won't, our expanding *noösphere* catch up with the expanding universe?

LaRouche: Well, actually, we are all part of the universe. All of us are. The meaning of our existence is of that nature. What do we contribute, by our existence, by our development, by our practice and development? What do we contribute to the totality of mankind? In the recent event we had on Thursday, we had a test of that on a large scale for China. We got involved deeply with some of what the Chinese development is.

So, the recognition of this thing which actually unifies humanity, in effect, as the demonstrations and the arguments and the proceedings showed—that is where mankind is. Mankind has to find its own identity, which means different kinds of inspections. But they all must come back to one thing, and that one thing is *the power of mankind*, the power of the human individual, when realized. That is the one thing which unifies all people: the ability to access a common progress for a better future for the totality of mankind, and mankind's mission for the universe.

Contributing to the Future of Mankind

Question: Good afternoon, Lyn! I'm from the Detroit area. I'm a veteran. I belong to at least three veterans groups, and I was wondering why there aren't more veterans gravitating toward the organization and what we do here? Because you're working toward preventing a number of future wars. And what is it that you think we can do to persuade more veterans to be involved with what we are doing?

LaRouche: First of all, you can start with Franklin Roosevelt, because Franklin Roosevelt was treated like a bum in the closing period of his life. He was one of the greatest thinkers in the history of the United States, in terms of the effect of what he contributed to a mankind which had been going into desperation, and now was reconstructing itself, where people in the early 1930s were totally into despair. Just the ordinary citizen was usually in total despair, or was a thief otherwise. And what happened is, Franklin Roosevelt brought that citizen,— who was often demoralized by what he had been subjected to, to cause him to aspire, to accrete to something which is going to be greater for the purpose of mankind, generally. And what has happened since is that those in the system of government, certain people in the system, have become no damned good at all. So therefore, we had so many no-damned-good candidates for leadership, in the United States, that we are sometimes ashamed of ourselves without asking and finding out why!

But that's it. We have to fight for that purpose. We have to understand what the meaning of that purpose is, of mankind. Not just for soldiers, because every one of us is going to die. And therefore the question is, what is the meaning of our living in the process which we know is going to end with dying. That means that you are looking at humanity, not as an object. You are looking at humanity as something which has an intrinsic continuity in terms of the contributions. For example, what happens, people talk about life and death. Well, everyone dies. Every human being dies. It's unavoidable. Well then, what is the purpose of the person having lived? That is the question. It's not how we die, it's how *we*, in the process of our existing, have contributed, and are continuing to contribute, to the meaning of the

"Einstein's role was a dedication to a discovery of the future," a future for the improvement of mankind even beyond the end of his life. Here (front row, center) he is at the 1927 Solvay Conference, at which the attack on him intensified.

future of mankind. And that is probably the simplest way of saying it.

Question: Hi Lyn, Alvin here. I did a fair amount of work leading into the conference, and what I was really inspired by, and at the same time embarrassed by as an American, was the international participation on the panel, and the excellent ideas and representations of where they see their nations leading to, and, of course, in essence, asking the United States to not wage war, but join them in that process.

But what I come out thinking today is, where do we go next? Where do we advance? What's our next move here in Manhattan, as an extension of that process that was in three parts presented to us on Thursday? And my thinking here in New York is that we have the release of these documents called the Panama Papers; we also have what will obviously be a widely seen broadcast on "60 Minutes," where the 28 pages will be gone through with many of the people that this organization has worked with and helped organize; and then later in the week we have "Fred and Ethel," otherwise known as Bernie and Hillary, coming into town. I'd like to know from you how we should approach this week, since there is a lot for us to do around this, and the implications are vast.

LaRouche: I would say that, with some brief exceptions, relatively speaking, among Presidents and among others, even most people, they are not worth much, at all. You know, you have to look at the question, as I do, from the standpoint of what is the meaning of a newborn baby? One that is going to live, or that we expect to live. Why do we put a value on that child? Because it is supposed to be, not just living for a while, it is supposed to be able to develop, in its self development, through mankind. We bring the baby, the child, or the fortunate child at least, into a role which mankind has never achieved before. In other words, the idea is to bring the newborn baby to be not merely a continuation of the parent, as such. The question is, can this baby, this person, represent the future of mankind in the course of its own existence? That's the important thing! Having a baby is not what's important, as such. What's important is creating a system which creates babies and makes babies into future geniuses!

Einstein, for example, typifies that model. And for many

White House Historical Association/The Peace Makers by George Peter Alexander Healy

Lincoln was one of the few people who created "a future for the improvement of mankind." Here Lincoln with General Sherman (far left), General Grant (center left) and Admiral Porter (right).

of us today who understood the history of Einstein, and his problems, Einstein has always meant that, for us who understood this. That Einstein's role was a dedication to a discovery of the future, *even when he would have died!* Therefore, his existence is a permanent existence, because it represents something which has never been overturned. And others should learn from his example.

Question: Mr. LaRouche, this is R— from Bergen County, New Jersey. You're talking about the issue of genius, and you mentioned Einstein. Einstein existed from the late 19th through middle 20th Century, and, as I see it, the objective conditions surrounding Einstein weren't necessarily great. There was World War I, there was anti-Semitism, he had to move from Germany to New Jersey. And yet he was a genius, there's no doubt the man was brilliant. And there have been many other cases of genius, people who have done their great work under adversity. We all know specific cases.

My question is, there seems to be a need for the cultivation of genius as a higher proportion of the population right now, and going forward. How do you visualize, how do you see a system, which would optimize or better grow this need for genius?

LaRouche: Take the history of genius in terms of

the United States, and take the founding leadership of the United States as such. Then look at what happened afterward. We had Presidents; we had a whole string of Presidents who were really treasonous, in terms of their attitude about the nation.

Then you had other people who came back, a few of them, as leaders, in terms of the development of the United States. Beyond Lincoln, we had a few people who actually filled that kind of role, of being a person whose life is devoted to creating a future for mankind. Not just a future for mankind, but a future for the *improvement* of mankind.

Now, what happened was that you had an evil bastard, I use the term freely, who became Bertrand Russell. And what Bertrand Russell did, he succeeded in getting at most of the people who were then at that time considered scientists, and they all turned rotten, every one of them.

And Einstein was the only man who really furnished the policy of honesty, in the development of the future of mankind and mankind's future. Some other people have made contributions, but we want to talk about a systemic approach to the improvement of mankind and mankind's destiny.

This is not just a step of progress. We have turned

back to evil, which was brought in by Bertrand Russell. And most people in the United States today are still worshippers of the policies of Bertrand Russell. They're still following—the schoolteachers, university student teachers, in the United States today, are mostly Bertrand Russell followers. They believe in simple mechanics, in terms of science. They have no creativity whatsoever.

And therefore what we treasure is the idea of having children being born, and knowing that those children will become something new and great beyond what has existed now, to hope that mankind will accede to actual progress of the development of the individual member of society. And that has been very much in jeopardy, and that's what is in jeopardy all the time. And that's what I like to fight about.

EIRNS/Philip Ulanowsky

We treasure "the idea of having children being born, and knowing that those children will become something new and great beyond what has existed now, to hope that mankind will accede to actual progress of the development of the individual member of society" which is in danger, "and that's what I like to fight about." Here, Dr. Robert Moon conducting a science class with students.

A Child Is Born … and Becomes a Genius

Question: Hello, Lyn, This is M— from Montreal. I've been able to work here for three weeks to help with the second Handel *Messiah* concert and the conference. Something I've been struggling with, that I hope you can help out with, is that practicality has been something which we all tend to fall into, and there's a lot of pressure to bring truth into practical terms, terms that people who don't know anything can understand.

But the idea of actually winning, the intention to win, I realize that has not been something—for the years I have been doing this—that I have not had governing my world. And that, in general, the way I have been thinking, wrongly, has been that I have been trying to inoculate people against the evil of the culture, at best, but the idea that you can actually win has not been, until very recently, a living concept organizing my mind.

Now this is completely different, especially for me. Being a part of this conference is a paradigm-shifting process. I know that if practicality was governing the minds of a Benjamin Franklin or a Brunelleschi, not only would there never have been a dome, but there never would have been a Renaissance, and there never would have been a Declaration of Independence. So, I am hoping you can say a few words to help people like myself and others to not fall back

into practical terms, and to keep their minds focused on self organizing processes.

LaRouche: I would say that's commendable, I think it's necessary. The thing to do is look at the idea of the concept of the baby, the human baby, and look at the meaning of what that human baby's birth *should mean* to humanity. It means that that child, or some children like that, are going to become a legion of people, from whom a future of mankind will be newly created, beyond anything that mankind has achieved previously. Therefore, the idea of the existence of the new baby must be, in some degree, a sample of a future of mankind; where the future of mankind has been reached, in a certain touch, that someone becomes the genius. A child is born, and in due course becomes, for one reason or another, a kind of a genius, and contributes to mankind what mankind has never acceded to before. And that is the thing which we should call "happiness," or "the meaning of life."

Question: Good afternoon, Mr. LaRouche. R— from Brooklyn here. I was at the conference this week and I was glad to see the progress the Egyptians have made in the Canal Zone. The United States Merchant Marine in the 1970s had a proposal for a two way system, and Egypt's participation in the New Silk Road is key to North Africa and Southwest Asia and humanity at large. Do you feel humanity will be able to overcome the effects of the British Empire to stop the Silk Road project?

LaRouche: I think we are, some of us, at least, determined to make that improvement permanent. Not only possible, but permanent. Not everybody will do it, will achieve it, but a great part of mankind can achieve it, and that will be good enough for the rest of them.

Question: It's me, Kesha. As I was sitting here listening, I was really struck by what you have defined as the necessity for the integrated, united, United States, and how that is being done with the representation of the Manhattan Project and New York as reviving the principle of Alexander Hamilton and what we're doing in Texas. And what struck me about that is, that we are really defining right now the fight against the slavery and anti human conception that has dominated our United States. And I think about this idea of the Hamiltonian Principle which acted as an anti-slavery idea against what we've seen in the Confederate South, and you've talked about the Confederate South a lot.

But the interesting question is, Why was it necessary that the space program be put in those areas that were a part of what was known or accepted as the Confederate South? It was because you had to give those people, those poor and backward regions access to their humanity. When people think about the space program, they think about it as some happy go lucky people making some scientific experiments. But I think about it from the standpoint that we have a responsibility of integrating the entire United States, and giving them access to their own humanity.

And I want to get your sense of that, because I think there's still a failed idea and conception, as to why it is so important that we integrate the United States and that this whole conception that has dominated the thinking and the population—the *slavery* that still exists! The South is still backward, and we're actually organizing to restore the principle of a unified United States—something that no one else is thinking about—but this has to be the method by which we bring the United States and the world into one accord again. What do you think of that?

LaRouche: What do I think of that? I think you should probably just tell other people about things that you already know. At a certain point you participated in the program of the space program, and up to that point this was a fine experience. But suddenly Obama came

Scan courtesy NASA/Johnson

Obama shut down the space program, but we will revive it, and get more people involved. Here astronaut Eugene Cernan on the moon. The lunar module and lunar rover are behind him.

along, and Obama shut down the space program.

Now today, you happen to be in a key position for fostering the revival of the space program. You're a leader in the space program. And therefore you're going to do more to try to reach out to get more people involved, in it. We'll even allow people in California to participate in the space program. These are the nice things that we can probably offer.

But the point is, that place is there! The same area that you were working in, when the space program was shut down, is still there. And we're now trying to struggle our way out from under the mud, to get into full and normal reaction to what the space program had meant in the beginning.

That was shut down by Obama. Now we're bringing it back. And now we know that we're capable of bringing it back and what we're going to do it to bring it back, and we're going to bring it back to the entirety of the people of the United States, among others, right now!

Question: Hello, Lyn. It's E— from Montreal, Canada. It's great to follow up Kesha. What I wanted to ask you: How does your concept of energy-flux density in the economy and progress upwards, translate into the moral domain of mankind? In other words, how does an individual in everyday life achieve better, more productive ways of contributing and participating in the universe?

LaRouche: I think it's better not to think of oneself as living in that kind of context. I think it's the idea of opportunity to get access, to create something for mankind, which is beyond what mankind has otherwise been able to get. And that's the simple foundation of things, that makes work good from failure.

Zealous Defense of Degeneracy

Question: Hello, Lyn. It's H— again from Montreal. I became involved with the organization about a year ago. Before that I was very much part of the degeneration and the ugliness of the culture, and finding myself here today, and the person I've become because of joining this organization and organizing myself, I struggle with fighting, as you say, with the Russell within myself and trying to find a way to inspire others to find the strength to fight that within themselves. And in particular, when it comes to youth, and the youth movement which you started for the future, as you mentioned, every week you're only getting older, and we're all only getting older, and the organization, a lot of the members are only getting older: So how can we, as an organization, find a way to fight, or to inspire young people, who are so zealous and adamant in defending the very system that is degenerating them?

And in particular, I know many young artists, very talented in terms of the technical aspects of art, but very depressed in why they do what they do and the reasons they do what they do. And for everyone watching this all over the world, and for here, how can we find a way to fight that zealousness within young people?

LaRouche: Fighting is a necessary occupation in these matters. For example, let's take Western Canada. A whole area, there, have been becoming suicide cases, where they had been enriched and progressive.

The question is, how do you answer that question? How do you account for that?

Now throughout the United States you'll find whole areas where people who were earlier progressively qual-

The Bertrand Russell influence is a force of evil, since the beginning of the Twentieth Century, wiping out the idea of creativity in entire generations. We have to "campaign to bring people to understand the importance of the human individual as a creative force."

ified people, suddenly become not only incompetent, but they become suicidal, *en masse.* They use drugs; they use other devices in order to get out of the experience of their life.

And this is true in much of the world. It's not just in these two areas, the phenomenon in Canada, which is significant, or the United States. And you go into the South, the southern states of the Americas. You see how desperate the situation is.

There's a force of evil, which I would locate as taking root, at the beginning of the 20th century, the Bertrand Russell influence. The Bertrand Russell legacy spread out throughout much of the world, throughout the trans Atlantic community and beyond, affecting, therefore, entire generations of people in these categories. We have to actually campaign, to bring people to understand the importance of the *human individual as a creative force.* And that's the only thing that will *do* anything for mankind, the asserting of mankind's role as a creative force, in the future.

Question: Hi Lyn, this is B— from New Jersey/New York and Los Angeles. I run into people just thinking on a lower level, object perceptions or sense perceptions. I think many of the qualities of this spiritual aspect of mankind [are found in Einstein]. For me, in just brief readings of Einstein's work, it really does give a sense that he was not a sense perceptual person. He did not believe in sense perceptions. It seems that in music it works pretty much the same way, if you do not believe in the notes, that is. Why is it that people just have a difficult time with this question of the spirituality of the human race?

LaRouche: Well, I don't find any problem in it. First of all, it's simple: You have to have a perspective. And the perspective is that you are going to do something to promote the creation and development of new human beings, and that you will have a part in the development of these new human beings.

We were supposed to educate children. Well, I can say that since Bertrand Russell came into power, we don't educate children any more, we downgrade children. We have had Presidents like Franklin Roosevelt and a couple of others who were creative, but most of our recent Presidents were trash or worse. Therefore, the struggle is to try to create an organization in society which gets rid of the trash problem; we call it the Bertrand Russell legacy. But most people have given in—most teachers have given in to this kind of thing, this treason against mankind. We don't develop creative minds seriously. Or if they are creative, we stultify their ability to express creative powers of development.

So I think that latter issue is the point which we ought to focus on, because there are many people who are wasting their entire lives by getting rich, and making the poor richer. That sort of thing.

So therefore, we should actually demand of ourselves that we take into account this kind of issue. And look at yourself from the standpoint of that kind of issue. What can you do to resolve your relationship to that issue?

Classical Composition Defines Creativity

Question: Hi, it's Diane. Yesterday at the conference, I was actually very struck by what happened in the Q&A period, because in the morning, we had Helga's speech; the Chinese representative discussing the One Belt, One Road; the speaker from Korea who was talking about the per capita income in Korea having gone from whatever it was, $100 per person, to being a major economy; the presentation by the Egyptian Consul on the extraordinary transformation and potential of that country; and then Helga's very distinct challenge to Americans to return to our Constitutional principles and the greatest identity of our nation.

Then when people got up to ask questions, it was as if this beautiful feast had been laid out before them, and they turned around to grab something out of the garbage can! It was like they stuck a banana peel on top of their heads and said, there's so much evil and I'm so oppressed."

So I was just very struck by this, and two things come to mind: One, a number of weeks ago, you emphasized the question of natural law, which I think is something that people don't have that great of an understanding of; and then also, the question of why the music work is so important in terms of dealing with this kind of phenomenon. Do you have more to say about this?

LaRouche: I will say it, because it's essential. This is essential. The composition of music, the way we are trying to bring it up to standard now, at this time, in this area, *that is what's crucial*. Why? Well, people say they

have all kinds of uses for what they call "music." But we know today, since the 20th century, most of what was called music became immediately junk! *There were no more great composers!* None! They were crushed. They didn't cease to exist, but they were crushed at every opportunity that institutions could crush them. Only a handful of people even approximated honest musical conceptions.

And you cannot separate that issue or issues from themselves. These things are important, and in their Classical compositional form, are intrinsically essential, if you're going to get a mind that is capable of understanding what music is. That's the thing to put on the plate right now.

That's the issue! You've got to be able to deliver Classical artistic composition, *alive!*

Question: [Renee Sigerson] Hello, Lyn. I was really struck yesterday when the professor on the final panel [Ben Wang] was showing the painting from China, and was discussing also the Chinese characters and the Chinese language—and that each character is monosyllabic, which really shocked me. It reminded me of the discussions we had on Classical Greek with Tony Papert, because the thing that suddenly hits you, when you're attempting to learn Greek, is that it's a language which actually functioned in the Classical period with the assumption that the person that you were speaking to had a mind! When we would work on this, I would really be struck, and say "you know the way we use English, we always assume that the person we're speaking to really doesn't have a mind!"

In terms of the functioning of the organization, part of the answer to what we're discussing here, is—and it's related to the pedagogy of music or like when we were just listening to the Furtwängler—that people have to really challenge themselves to hear the inner voice of the other at all times, that kind of discipline, and really get rid of this traffic-light way of having dialogue with people.

Because it's really not a question. I think what the Chinese example shows—because they have survived all these centuries, and discovered and rediscovered—is that what is metaphorical within language is something which is embedded in the process by which people live and work together. And there's such a strong emphasis in China on multi-generational survival, that obviously this is somehow embedded in what they're doing.

But maybe you can explain this better than I can.

LaRouche: There are several aspects of this question which you pose which I can deal with here; because some of it goes deeper, there. But I take it in terms of my own life. I succeeded several times in my life, and each time—coming out of military service, back into normal non military life was quite a difference—but I was then a victim of the evil forces that conjured this thing, and I battered around for a while, and I rose to a significance in the course of a generation; and I was put into prison. I got out of prison, and I got help in a sense, from Bill Clinton and others who sponsored my getting out of the prison system; and I went back into scientific work again, in Russia and other parts of the world.

So that's the way life sometimes goes. So the question is, what underlies the difference between one kind of experience and another? And the main thing, which lies within the human being, or one who's prompted to living, is that *Classical artistic composition, true Classical artistic composition* is the universal principle on which everything that's important is based. And I know it comes in different forms of expression, but I can say *Classical musical composition* is a paragon defining creativity. It's what the baby learns eventually, what the adult learns, and what somebody ends up producing.

Question: Hi Lyn. You mentioned a couple things that just resonated with me right now—the metaphor of the baby, and Classical composition. The first thing that went through my mind when you mentioned the baby was Plato's *Symposium* and the idea that we all are pregnant, either in body or in mind. How can this organization help all of us refine our ability to give birth to that child, metaphorically speaking, using the Classical composition? Using the Classical ideas of what humanity is, and what the spirit of humanity is?

LaRouche: Well, when there's been a cutoff of periods of creativity in the history of mankind, you find that there's a cutoff. And then you look around and you find that eventually somebody comes back and brings something new which is also creative.

So the design of mankind to become creative, to live as a creative personality, that is a driving force in and of itself. And often people will discover that in themselves, rather than discovering it from some other source. They simply decide themselves that they want to think and talk *in this way*. They want to communicate

Société Wilhelm Furtwängler
True Classical artistic composition is the universal principle on which everything that is important is based. Here, Furtwängler conducting in Paris in 1934.

in this way. They want to live in this kind of way! So sometimes, many people are successful, not the greatest number of people, but a great number of great people, are able to do that. And if they are influential and allowed to become influential, then it works.

If you get the kind of teachers that are trained under Bertrand Russell from the beginning of the Twentieth Century, then you get a stinking project! And a product to go with it.

That's been the problem. That's the problem we face when we talk about the question of the relationship of mankind to the future. There are people who are actually disgusting, they *do not* respect the principle of the future of mankind, that mankind must be motivated to find in himself and herself something of creativity, which gives them access to understanding something which is beautiful, and which they want to serve. And I think that's the only easy way to get a description of it.

Speed: I think we're at the end of the questions, Lyn. I think today's dialogue has been notable for several reasons. One if that we actually have a dialogue with Lyn and the Policy Committee, because we have Diane *and* Kesha here, and you have an audience for that dialogue made up of organizers, who've actually been qualified to be in it. This is a higher level meeting, I think, than we've had.

So, if you have anything else to say to us, please go ahead.

LaRouche: I should say, we should be more creative than you've ever been before!

Editorial

New Documents Further Detail Obama's Collusion with 9/11 Sponsors

April 19—The Interagency Security Classification Appeals Panel (ISCAP), the highest declassification authority in the Executive Branch of the U.S. Government, housed at the National Archives, has declassified 29 new documents relating to the government's investigations into the 9/11 attacks, and they reveal new, damning details about the Saudi Royal Family's deep involvement in those September 11, 2001 attacks.

From the time of his first campaign for President in 2008, Obama has promised the families of the 9/11 victims that he will declassify the 28 pages from the Joint Congressional Inquiry, which detail the Saudi involvement in those heinous attacks. He has not only broken that promise. Obama has consistently protected the Saudis from justice over their role in 9/11 and is now openly showing his hand by pledging to veto the Justice Against Sponsors of Terrorism Act (JASTA), now before the Congress, just prior to his now ongoing visit to Saudi Arabia. The President has sold out the American people to his slavish loyalty to the Saudis and their British patrons. This is a crime that demands, at minimum, President Obama's immediate impeachment.

The 29 documents now declassified, contain work sheets, interview notes, and other documents from the 9/11 Commission, that make clear that the Federal investigators probing the Sept. 11, 2001 attacks had compiled massive amounts of evidence of direct involvement by agents of the Saudi Royal Family, the Saudi Ministry of Religious Affairs, and the Saudi Ministry of Defense and Aviation. They provide a backdrop to the suppressed 28-page chapter from the earlier Joint Congressional Inquiry, which merely summarized the volumes of evidence compiled—and covered up—about the direct Saudi government complicity in 9/11.

Perhaps the single most damning document, declassified last year, is a 47-page memorandum by Dana Leseman and Michael Jacobson, detailing all of the Saudi government officials who were implicated in the 9/11 attacks. Leseman was a Justice Department attorney and Jacobson was an FBI Special Agent. Both had served as key investigators for the Joint Congressional Inquiry, and had authored the 28-page chapter that Presidents George W. Bush and Barack Obama have suppressed. They went on to work for the 9/11 Commission, where their efforts to pursue the Saudi leads from their earlier work were stymied by Commission director Philip Zelikow. Leseman was ultimately fired by Zelikow for refusing to obey his orders to stop the probe of Saudi Royals' ties to 9/11.

The 47-page document identified a total of 21 confirmed and suspected Saudi government employees who abetted the San Diego hijackers cell during the year-and-a-half that they were in the United States preceeding the Sept. 11, 2001 attacks. The document detailed all of their roles in supporting the two West Coast hijackers, Nawaf al-Hazmi and Khalid al-Mihdhar. It also called for a thorough investigation of the FBI, which had an informant in San Diego who housed the two 9/11 hijackers in his home for months before the attacks.

One of the central figures linking the Saudi regime to the 9/11 plotters was Omar al-Bayoumi, a Saudi intelligence agent who was the main financier of al-Hazmi and al-Mihdhar during their entire time in the United States. In addition to his no-show job, with a sizeable expense account from a Saudi Ministry of Defense and Aviation contractor, Dallah Aviation, al-Bayoumi earlier received $400,000 from the Saudi Ministry of Religious Affairs during the 1990s, ostensibly to build a mosque in the San Diego area. Investigators believed that those funds may have been used to build up terrorist cells in the area. These beliefs were buttressed by the fact that the San Diego mosque was run by Anwar Al-Awlaki, a spiritual leader of Al Qaeda, who was ultimately killed in a U.S. drone strike in Yemen—and who may also have been an FBI informant.

The evidence of deep Saudi involvement is almost matched in the 47-page document by evidence of FBI coverup of the 9/11 story. One segment of the recently declassified "Document 17" featured a series of questions about FBI stonewalling and coverup.

The document posed the following two questions: "1. Did the FBI intentionally withhold from the Joint Inquiry information about the informant's relationship with the hijackers and subsequently attempt to obstruct the Joint Inquiry's investigation of the matter?

"2. If the FBI did withhold information and obstruct the Joint Inquiry's investigation, were the FBI's actions indicative of a larger pattern of FBI non-compliance with Congressional oversight? What changes would therefore be needed to ensure more effective Congressional oversight of the FBI?"

A thorough review of all of the newly released documents is now underway. But sufficient evidence is already reviewed, proving the deep Saudi role in 9/11 and the ongoing coverup by President Obama and top officials of the FBI.

The evidence of President Obama's witting role in this coverup already meets and passes the Constitutional standards of "high crimes and misdemeanors" requiring impeachment proceedings. There are credible reports circulating in Washington that President Obama is using his current visit to Saudi Arabia to solicit funds from the Saudi Royals for his post-presidential library and career—perhaps in return for guarantees that the 9/11 story will continued to be covered up at the top. Is there any justification for delaying one moment more the launching of those long-overdue impeachment proceedings?